CARTOON CURVY ART BOOK

BY STEVE COFFIN

WRITTEN AND ILLUSTRATED
BY STEVE COFFIN

COPYRIGHT © 2016 STEVE COFFIN

ISBN-13: 978-1540336354 ISBN-10: 1540336352

DEDICATION

THIS BOOK IS DEDICATED
TO MY WIFE ALLYSON, MY FAMILY
AND CHILDREN LEE, ABBY AND CLEA.

ACKNOWLEDGMENTS

I WOULD LIKE TO THANK EVERYONE
WHO HAS SUPPORTED ME IN THE PROCESS
OF MAKING MY ART BOOK.
ALSO I WOULD LIKE TO THANK THE CAFE MULLIGAN
AND THE CAFE BRITISH FOR THE AWESOME
COFFEE AND FOR GIVING AN ARTIST
A PLACE TO WORK....

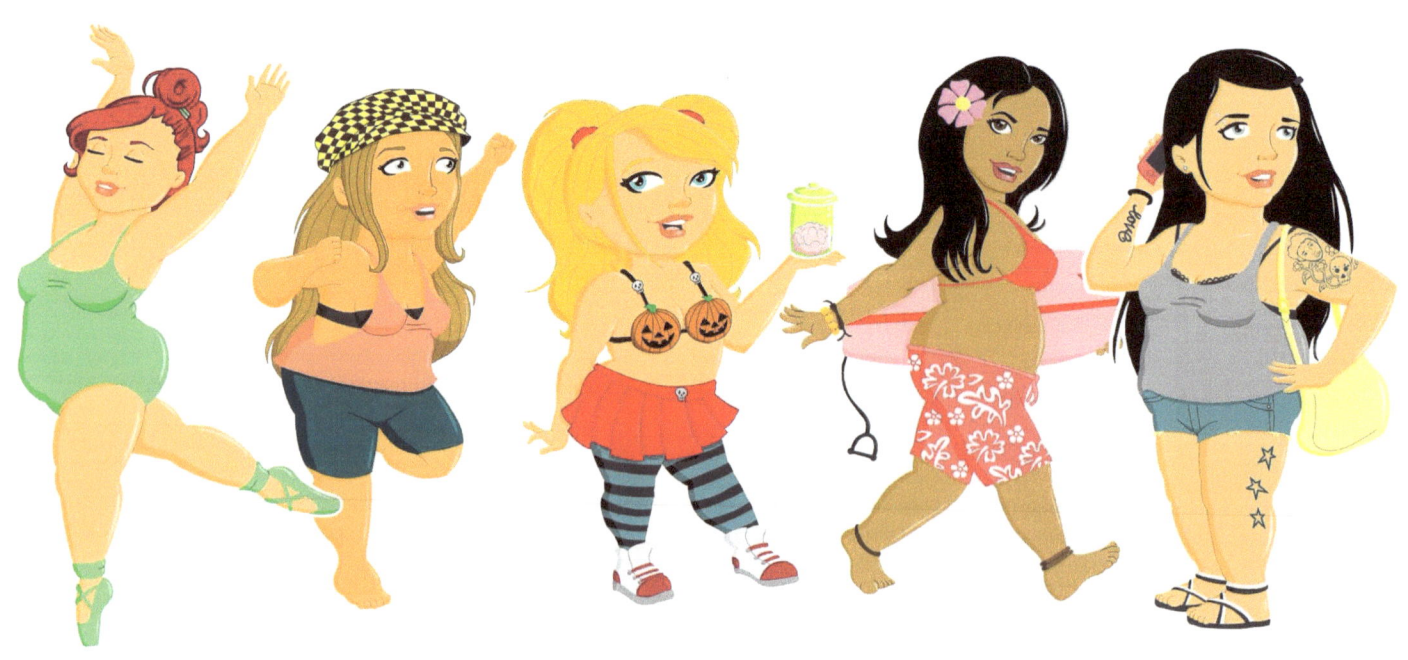

INTRODUCTION

THANK YOU VERY MUCH FOR PICKING UP MY ART BOOK
AND WELCCOME TO THE WORLD OF CURVY CARTOONS.

MY AIM WITH THIS BOOK IS TO SHINE A LIGHT ON
THE SUBJECT OF BODY POSITIVITY. THERE IS NO
WRONG WAY TO BE YOU AND WE SHOULD
ALWAYS START FROM A PLACE OF LOVE...

"THE WORD **PERFECT** HAS BEEN HI-JACKED. **YOU ARE** PERFECT
TO START WITH. YOU ARE THE ONLY EXAMPLE OF YOU
THAT THERE WILL EVER BE, AND THAT MAKES YOU UNIQUE,
AND THAT **IS** WHAT MAKES **YOU PERFECT**..." *STEVE COFFIN ©2016*

Steve Coffin 2016

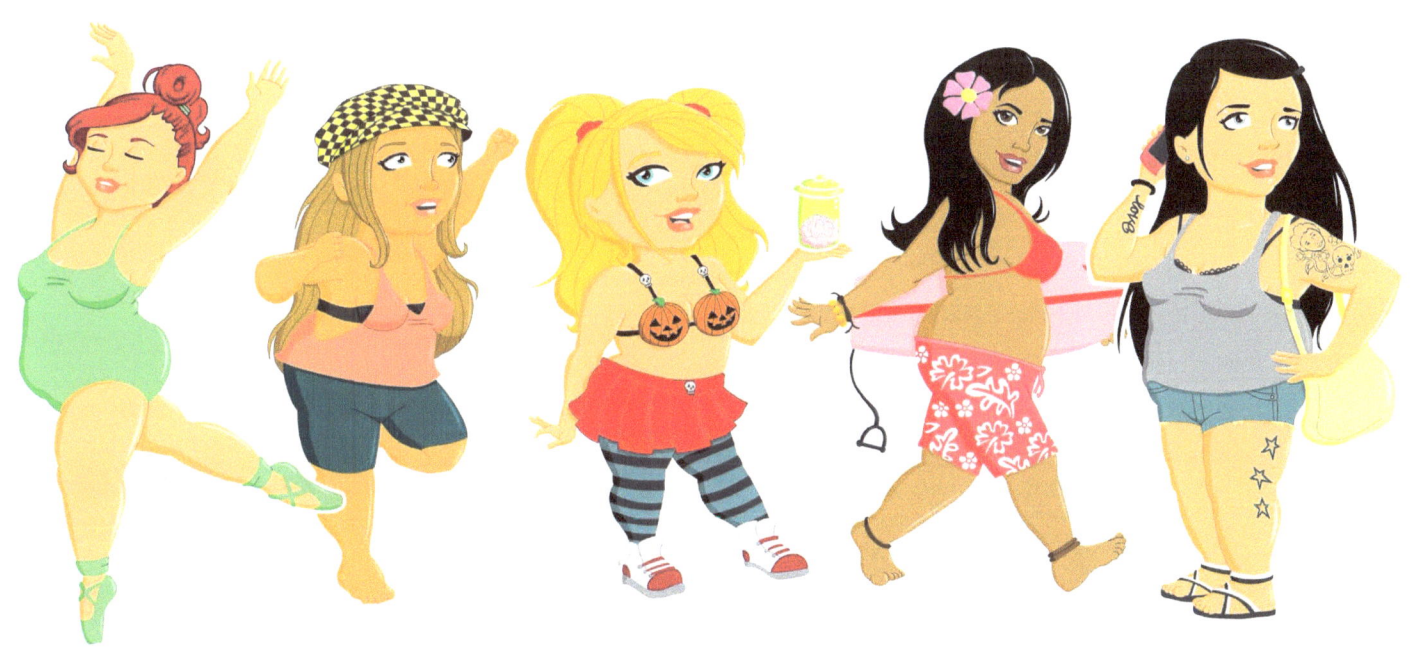

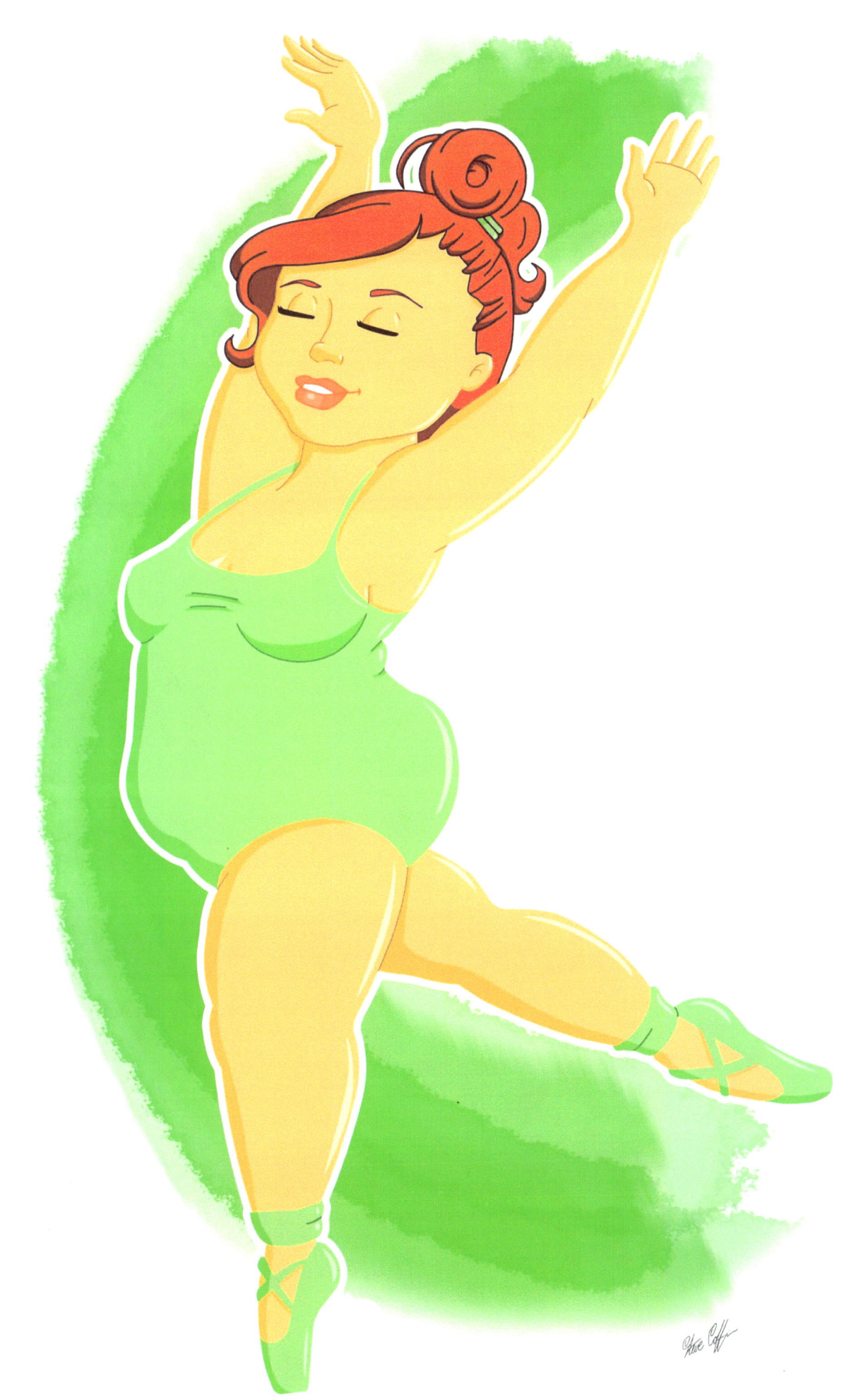

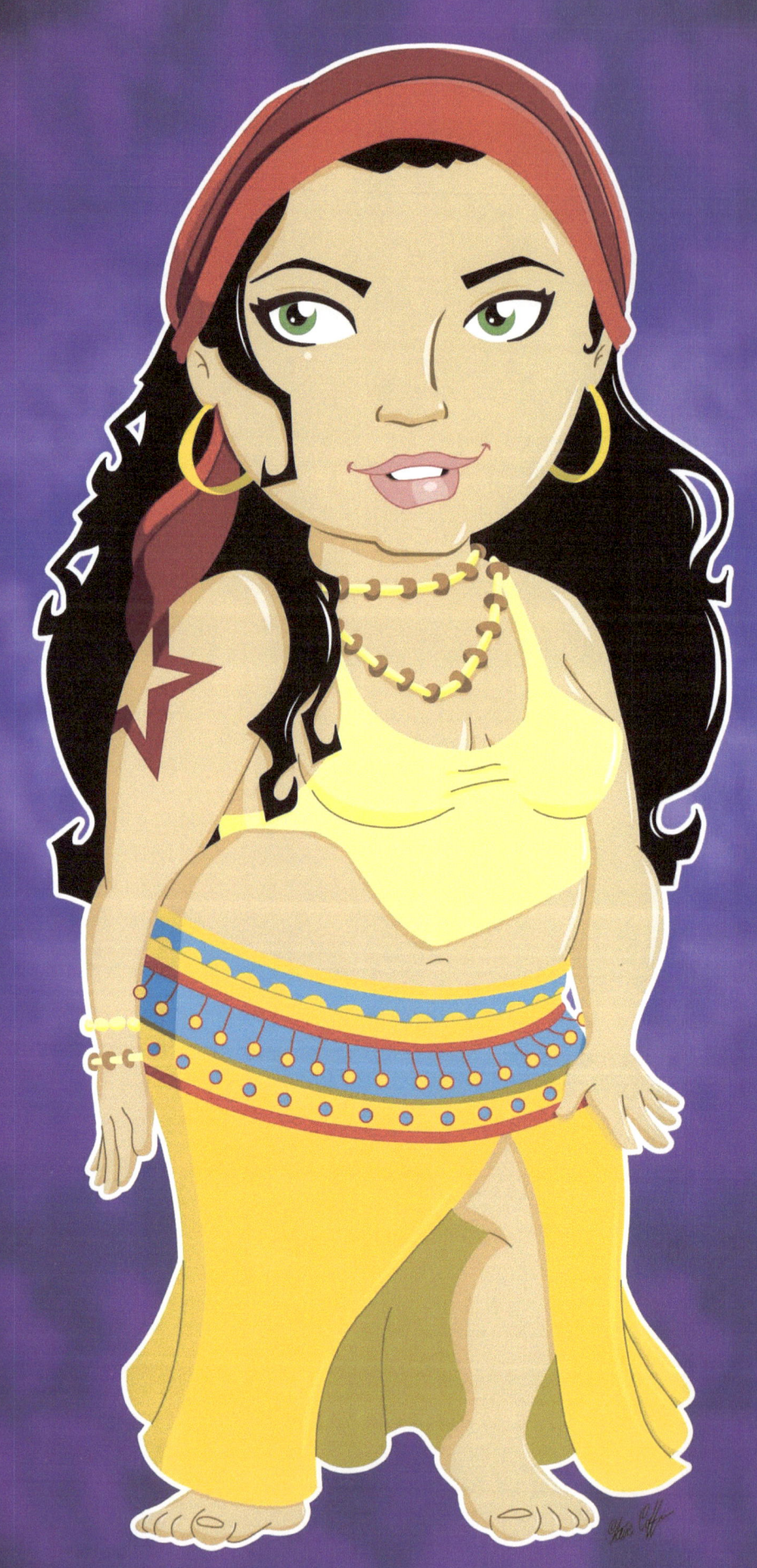

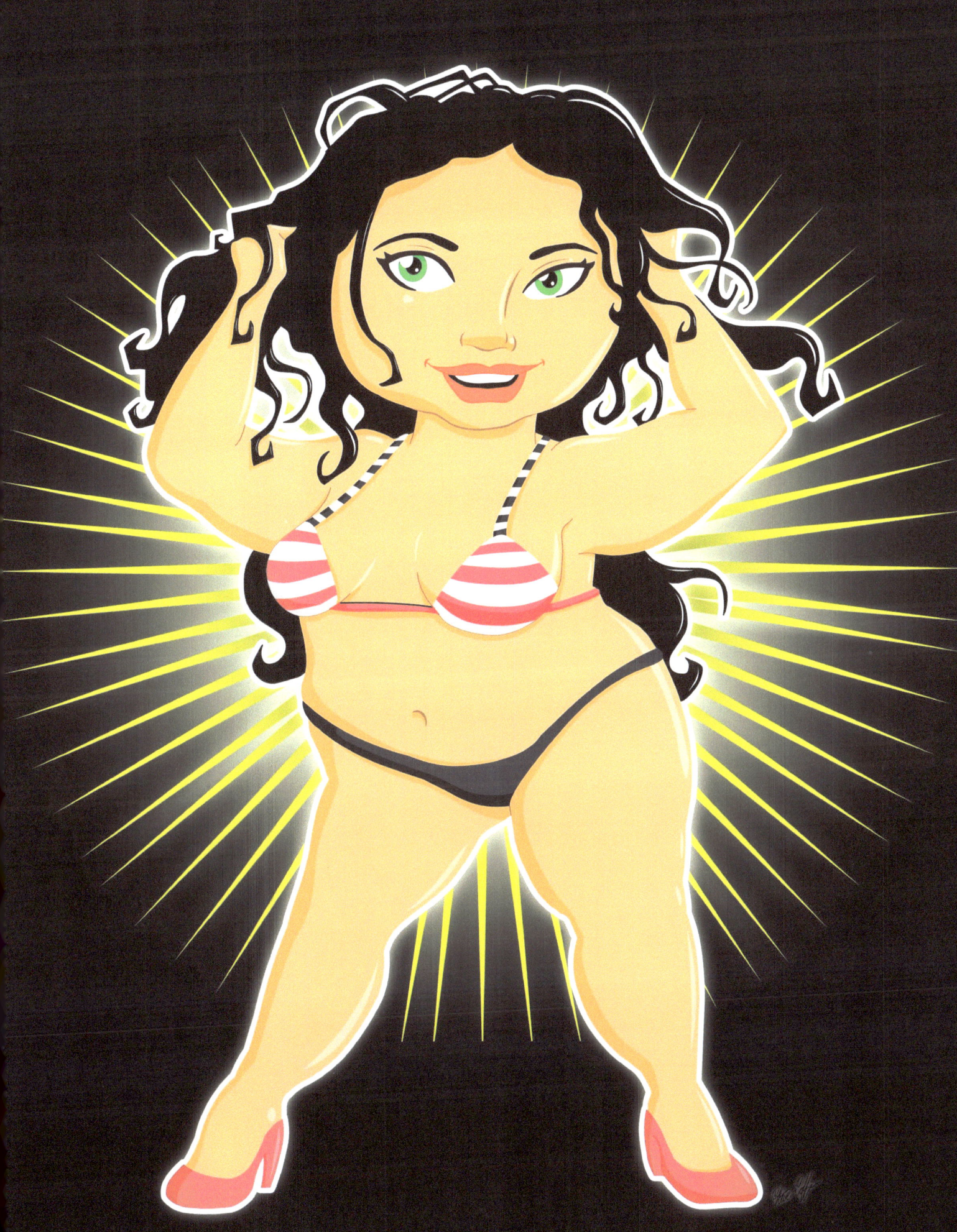

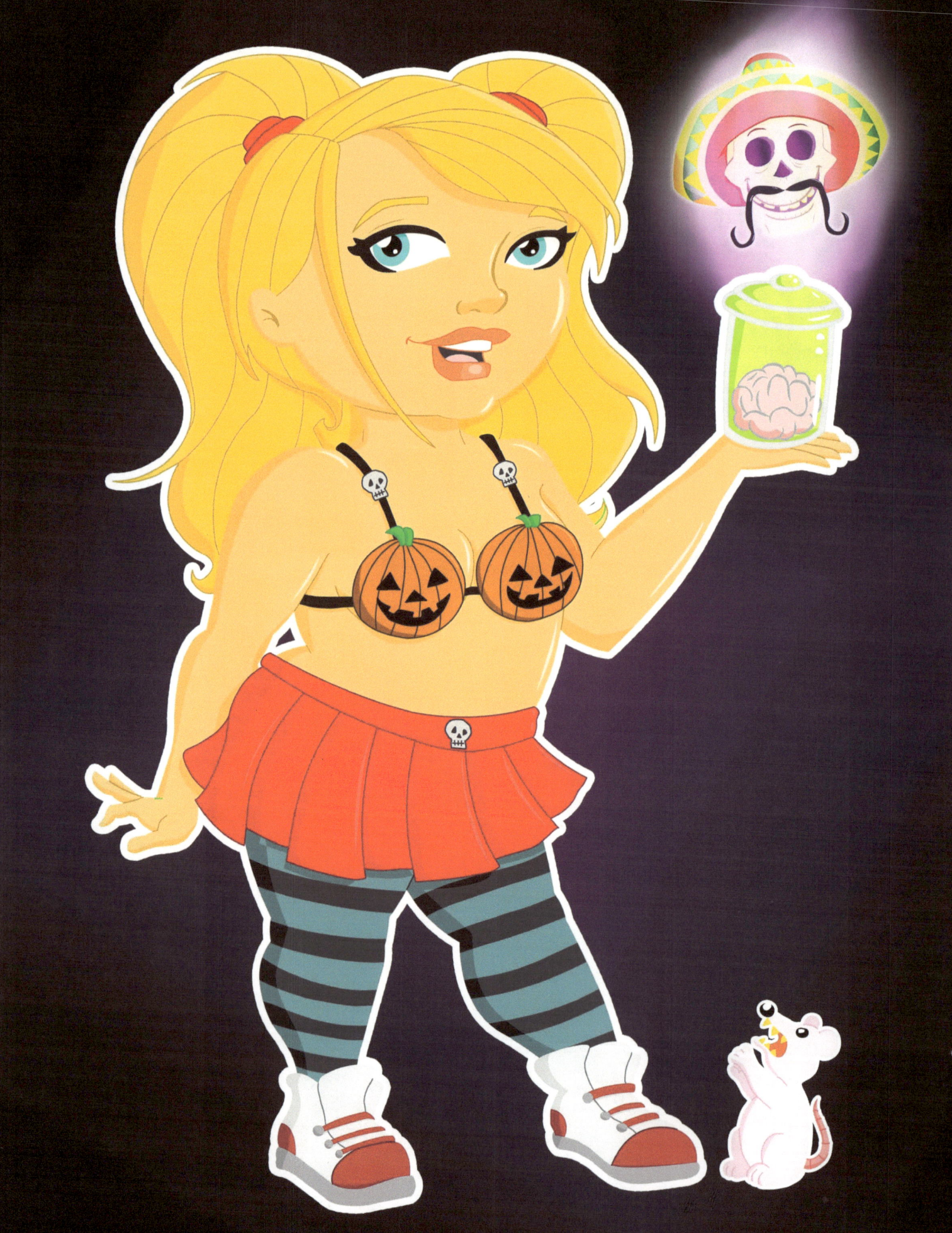

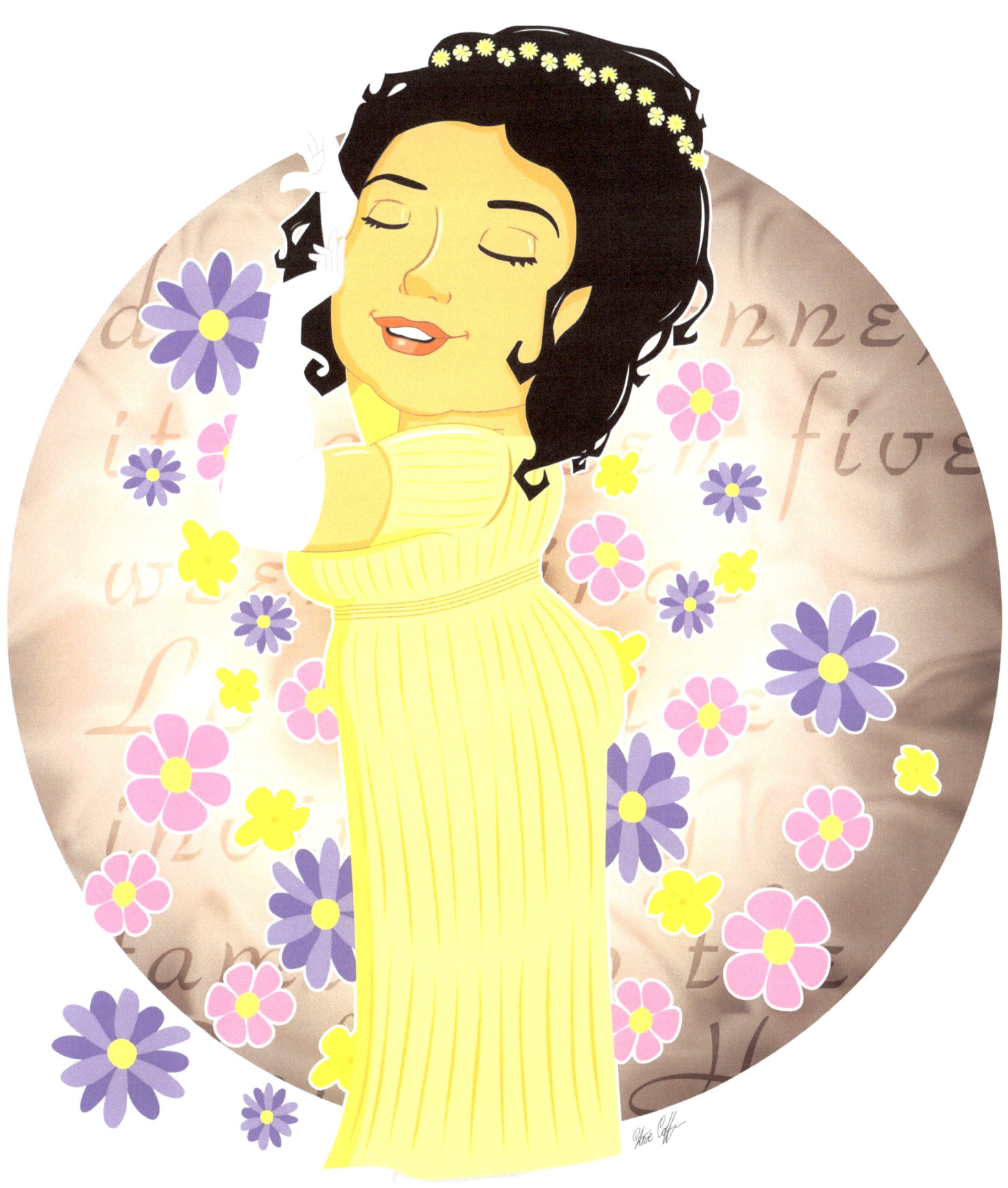

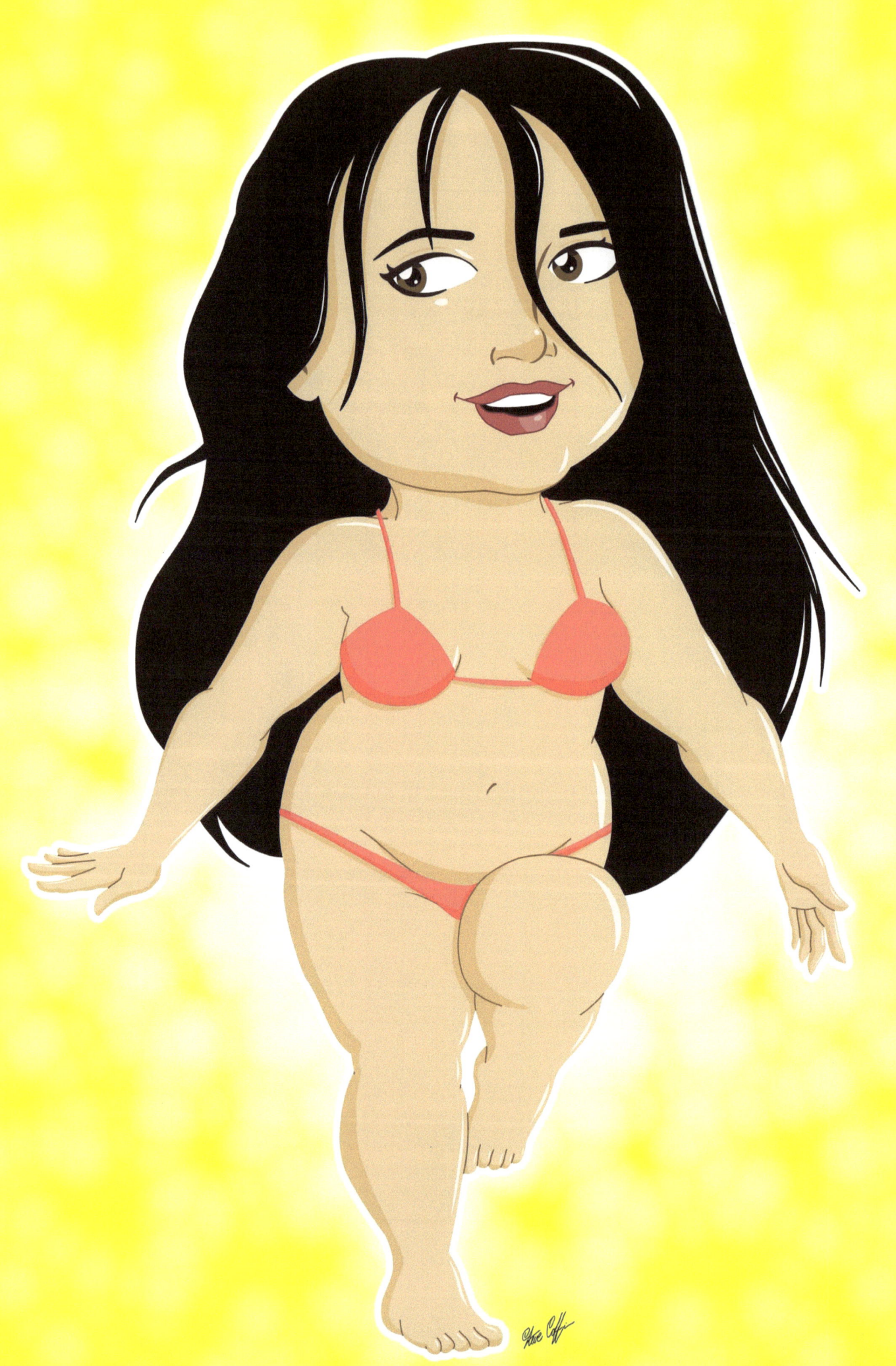

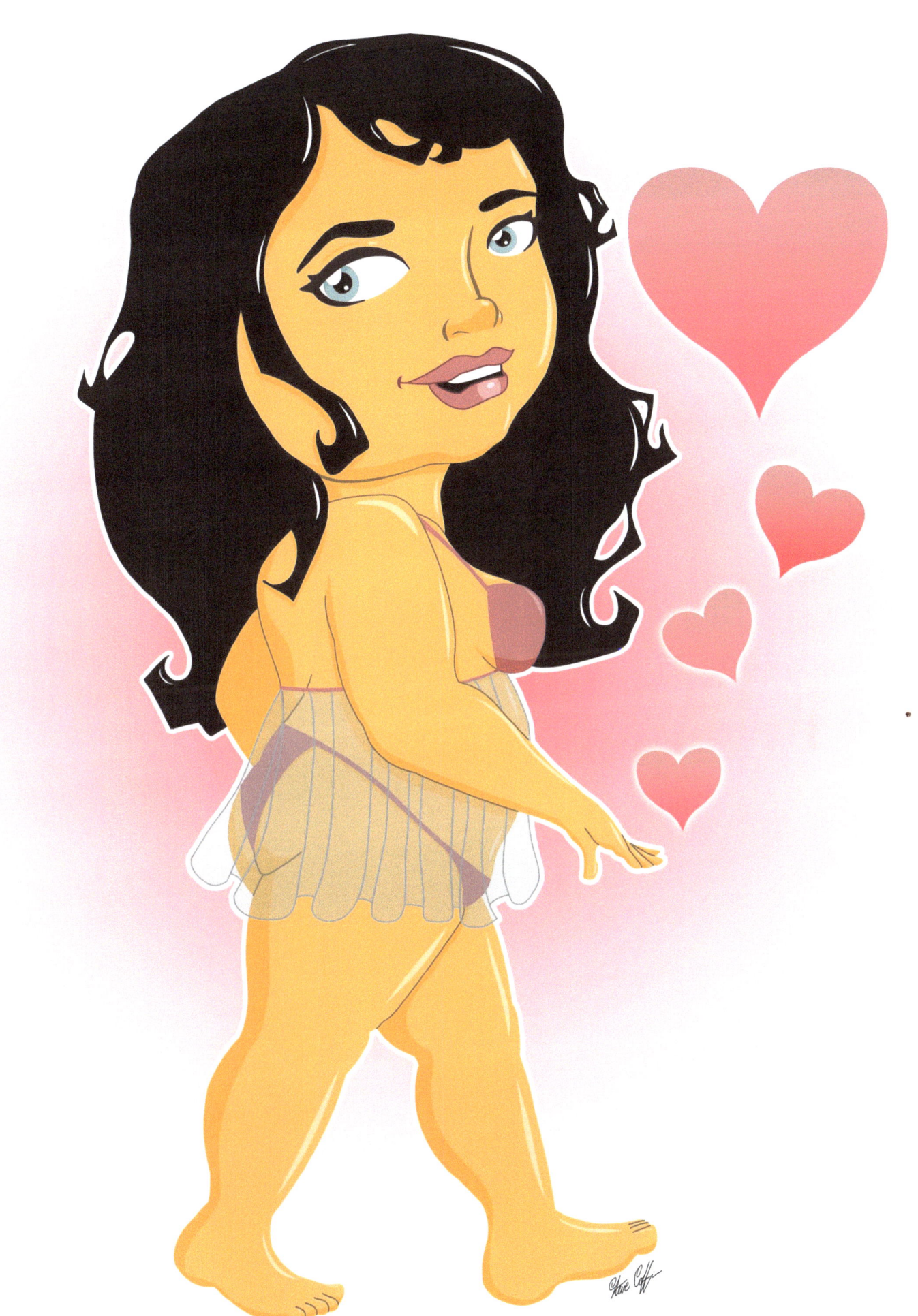

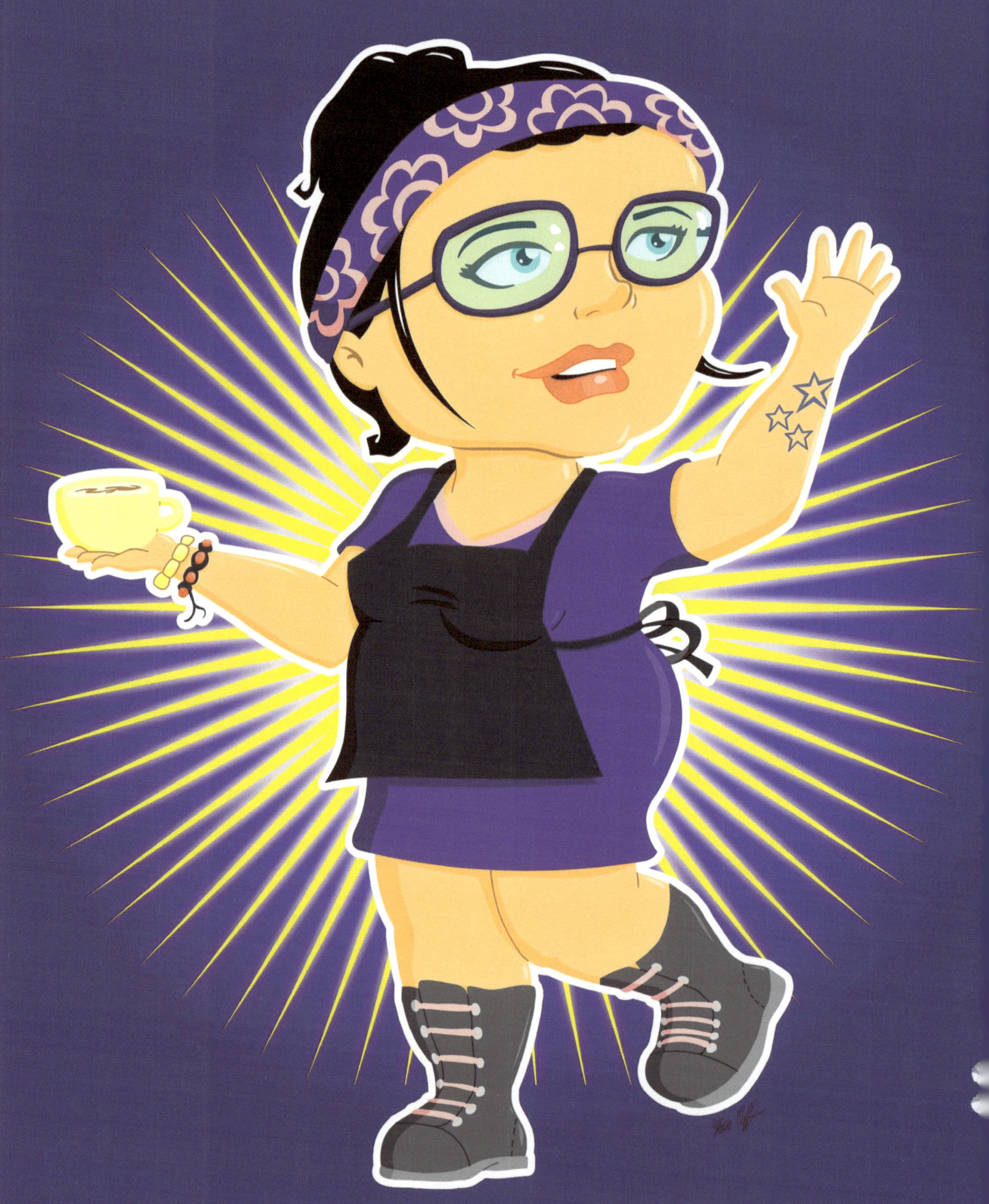

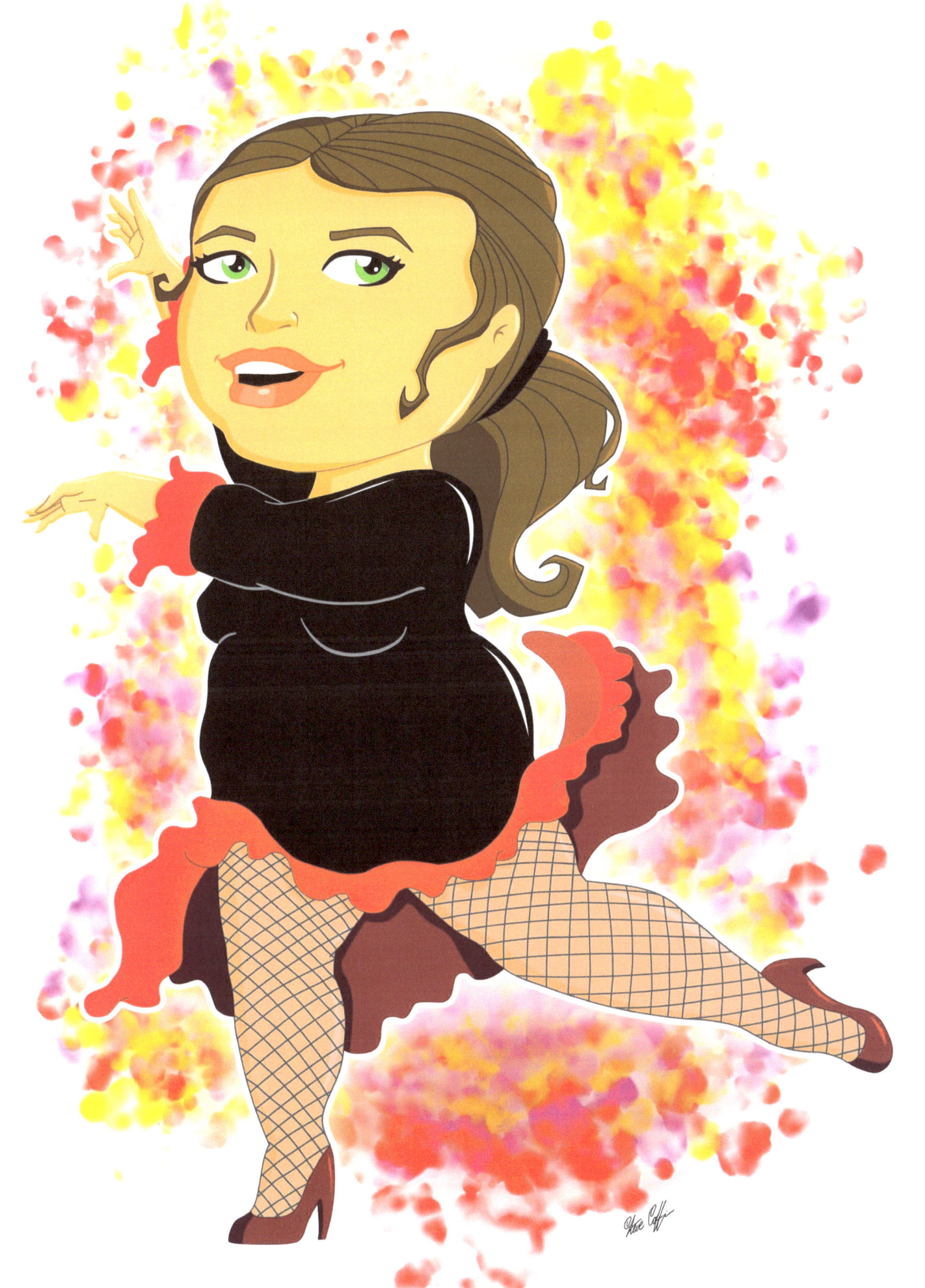

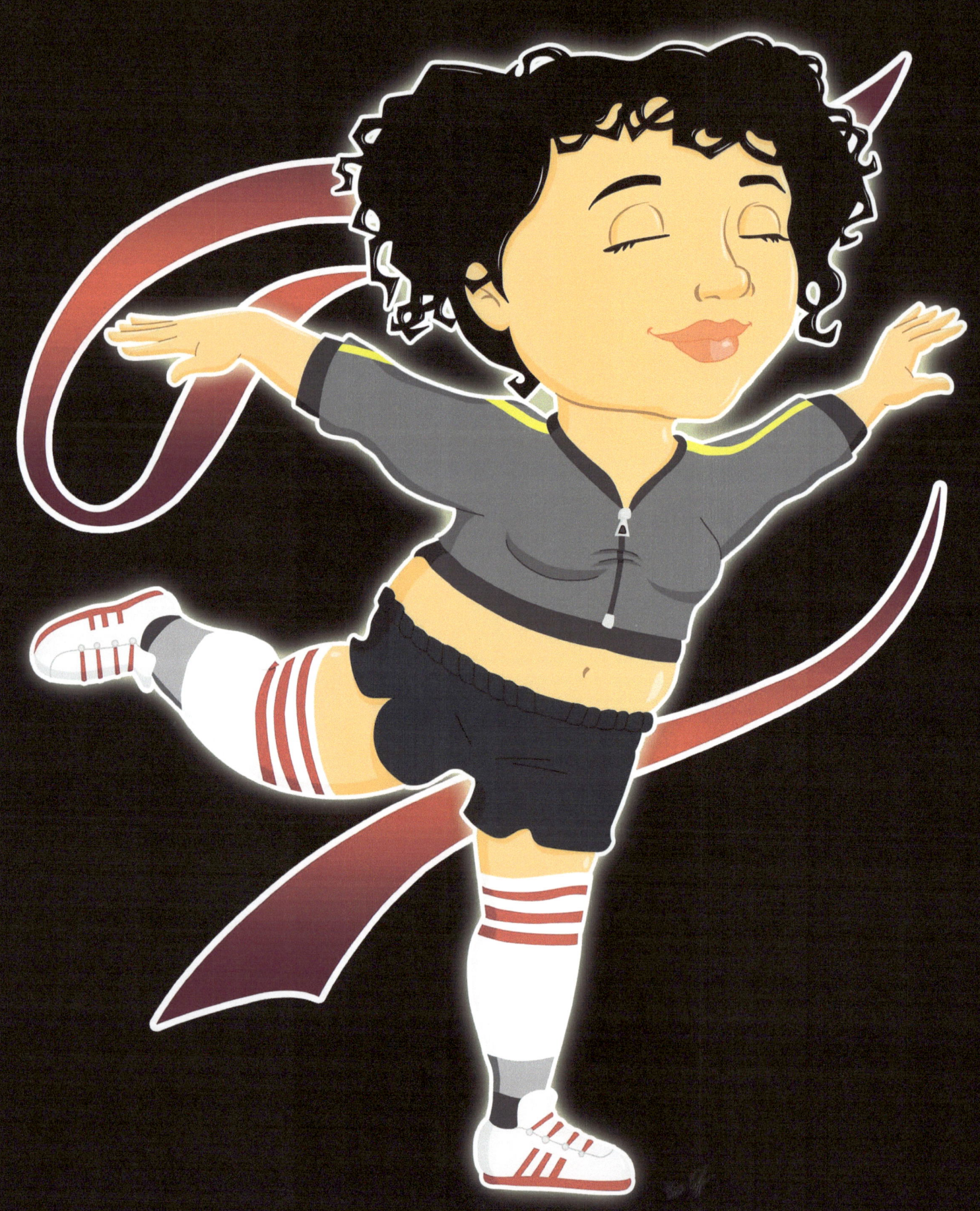

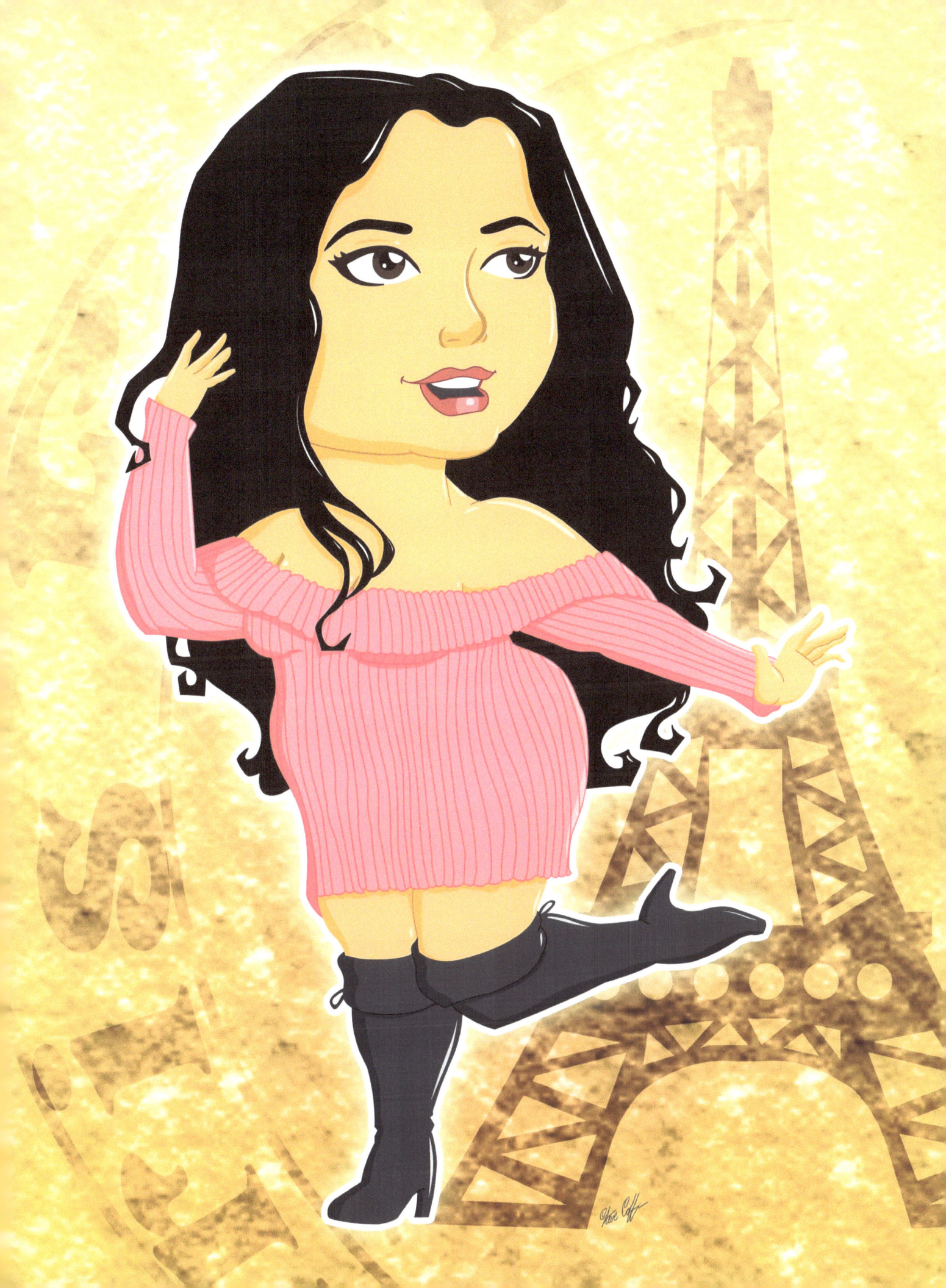

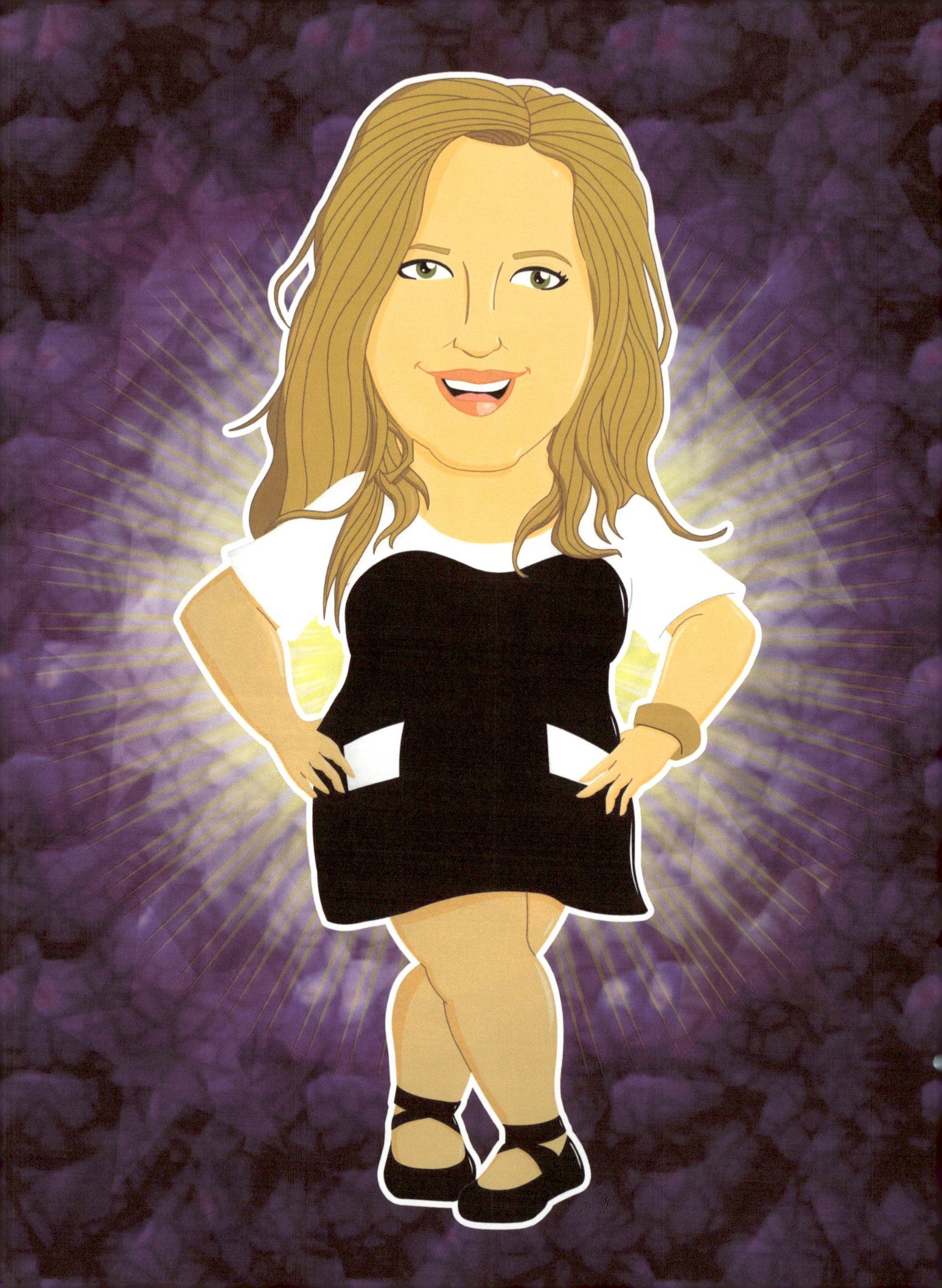

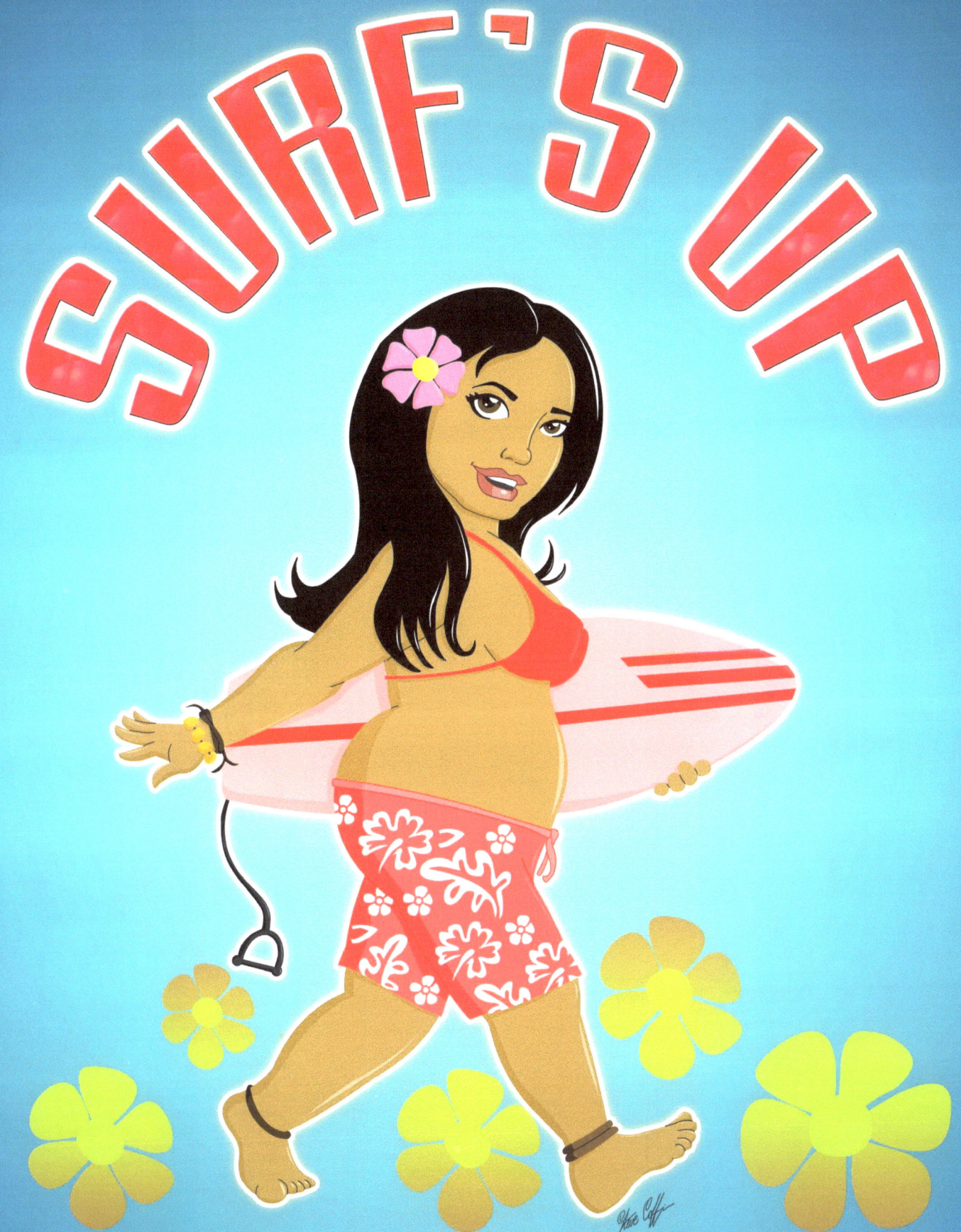

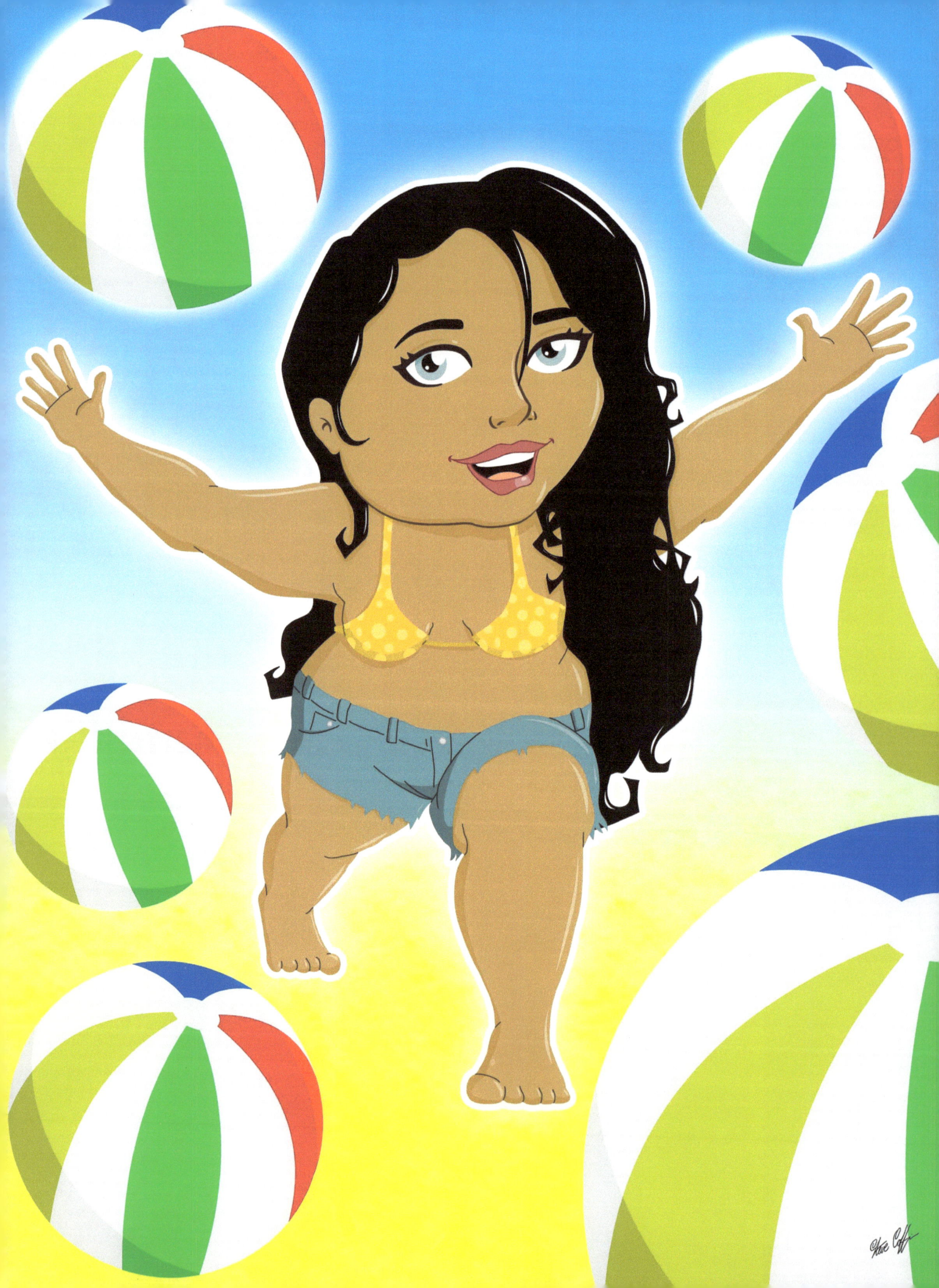

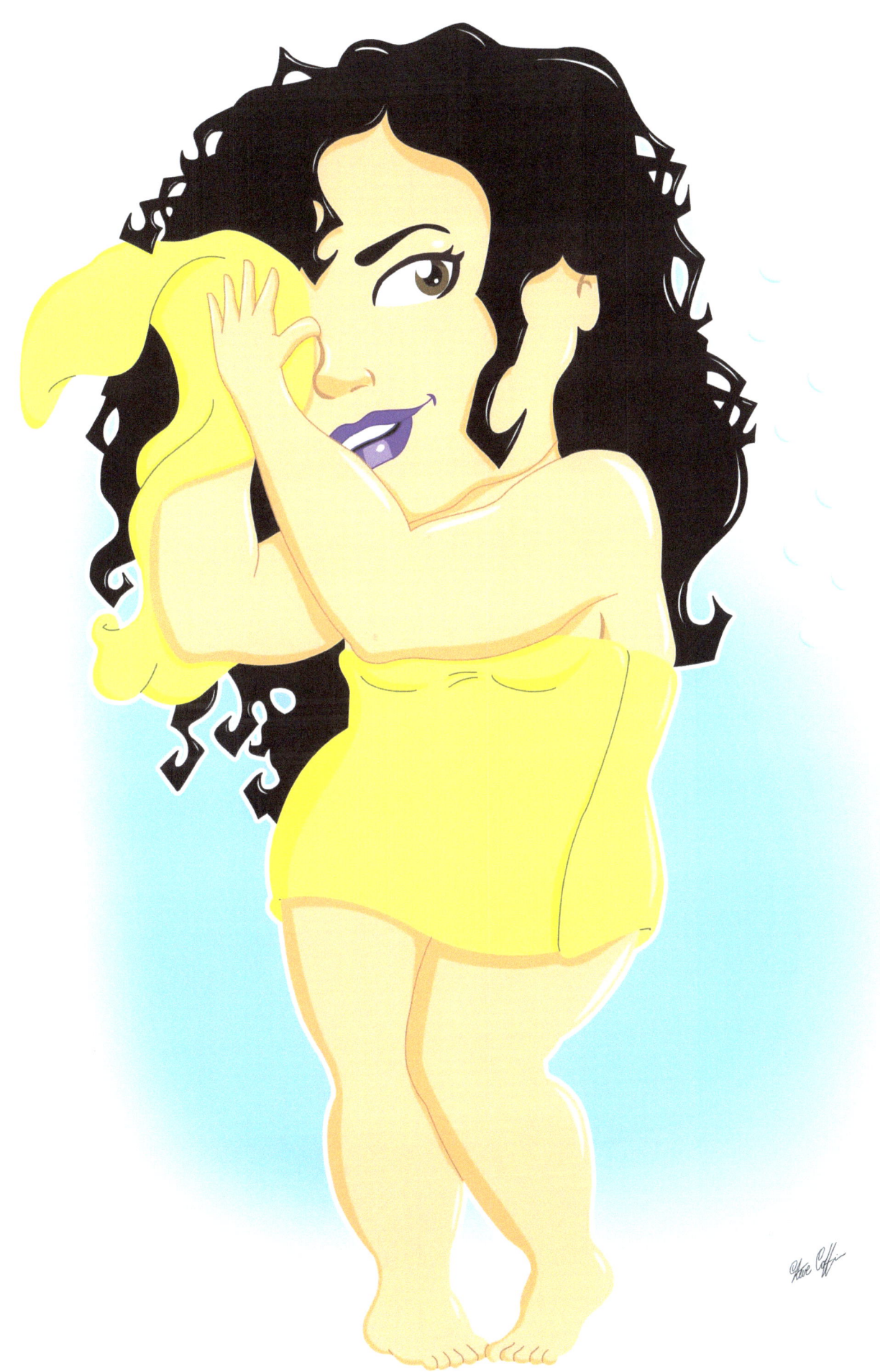

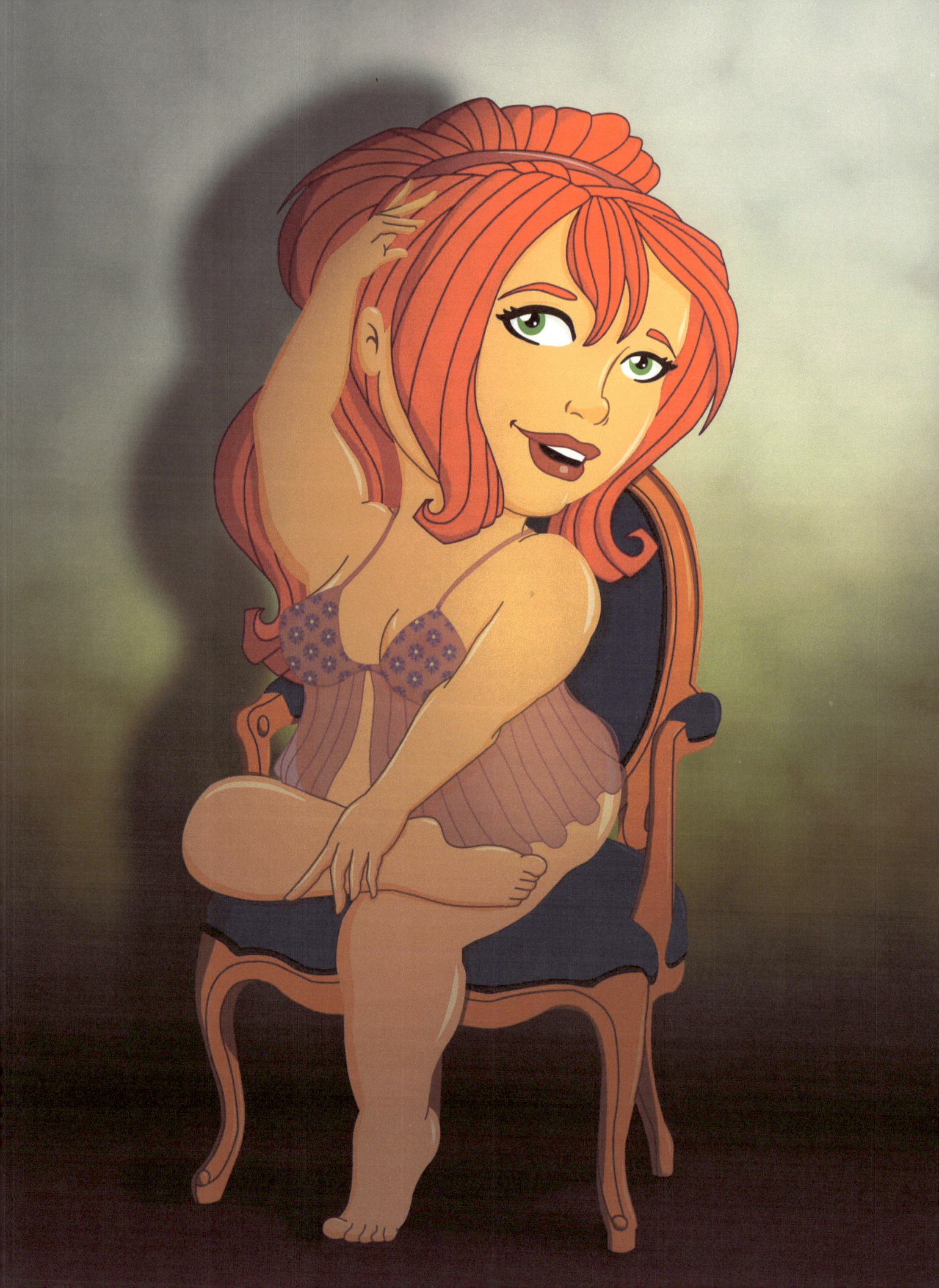

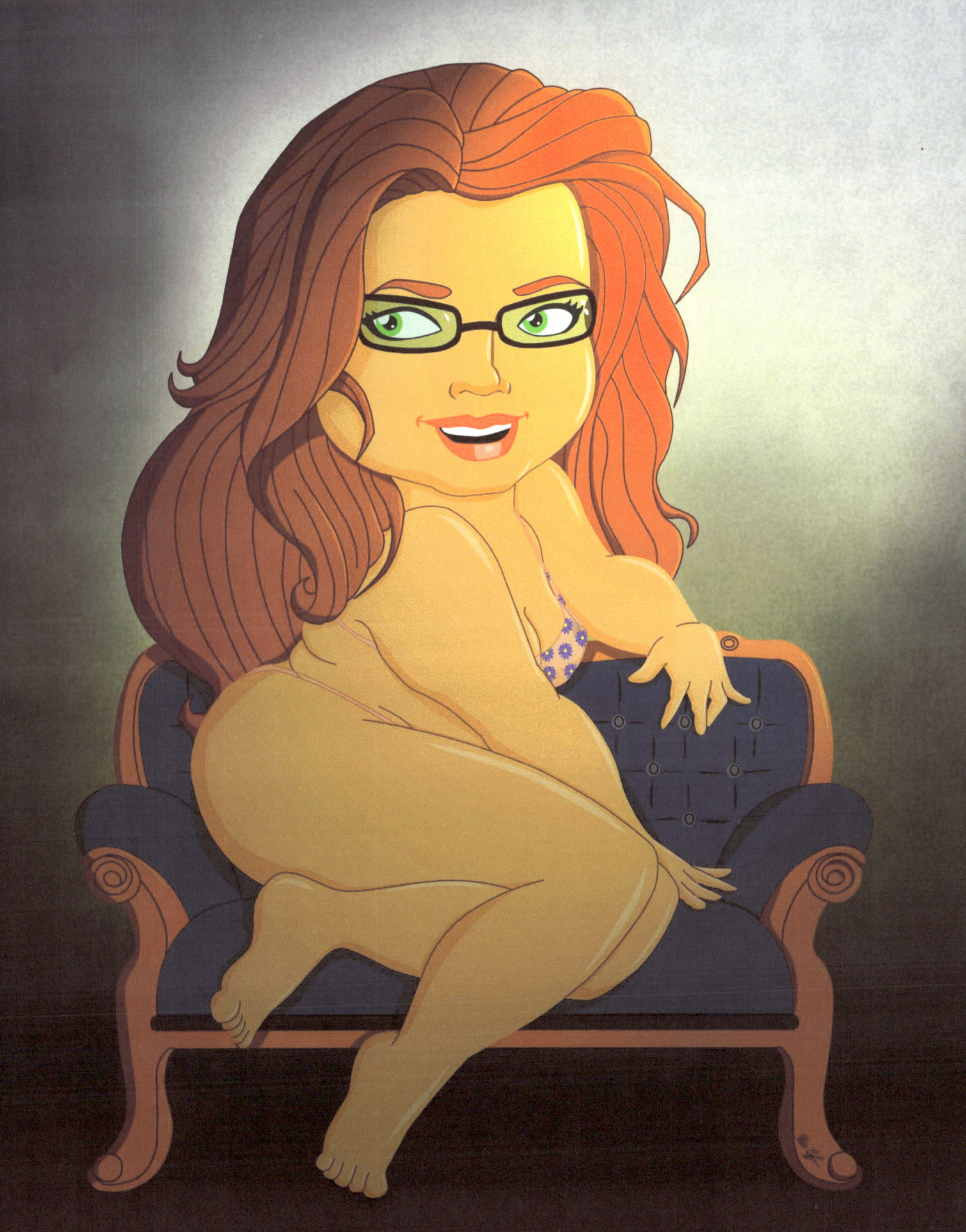

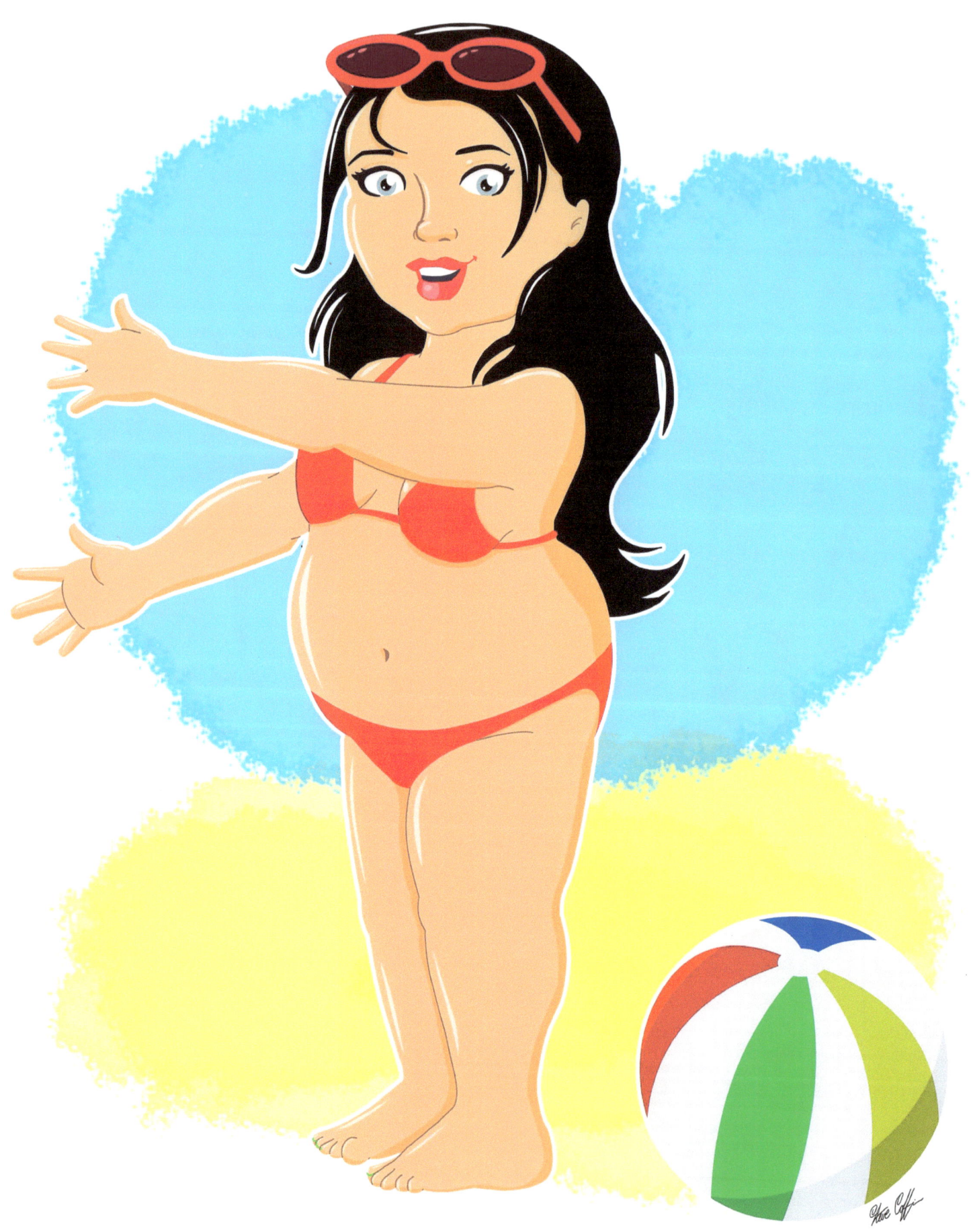

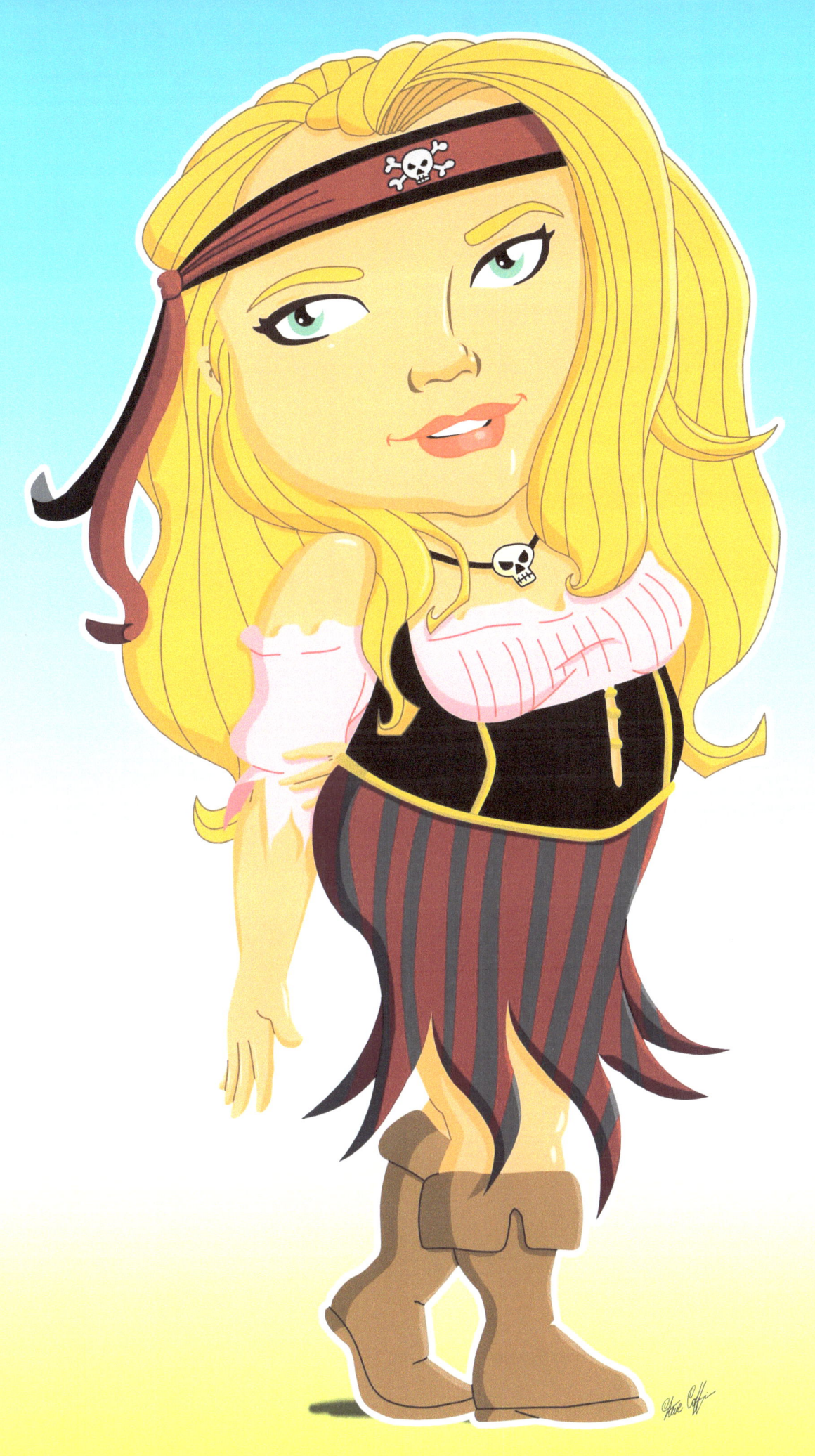

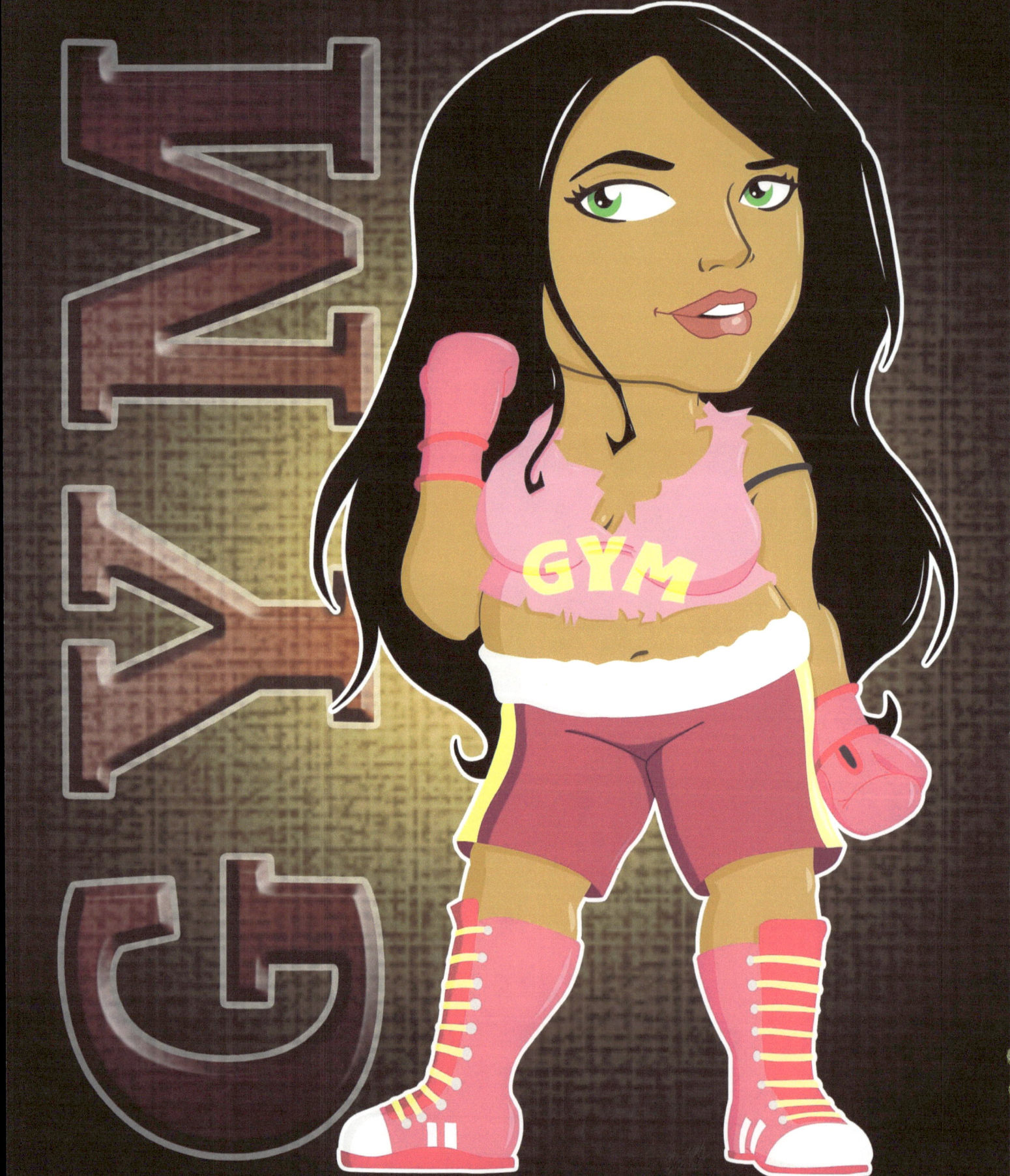

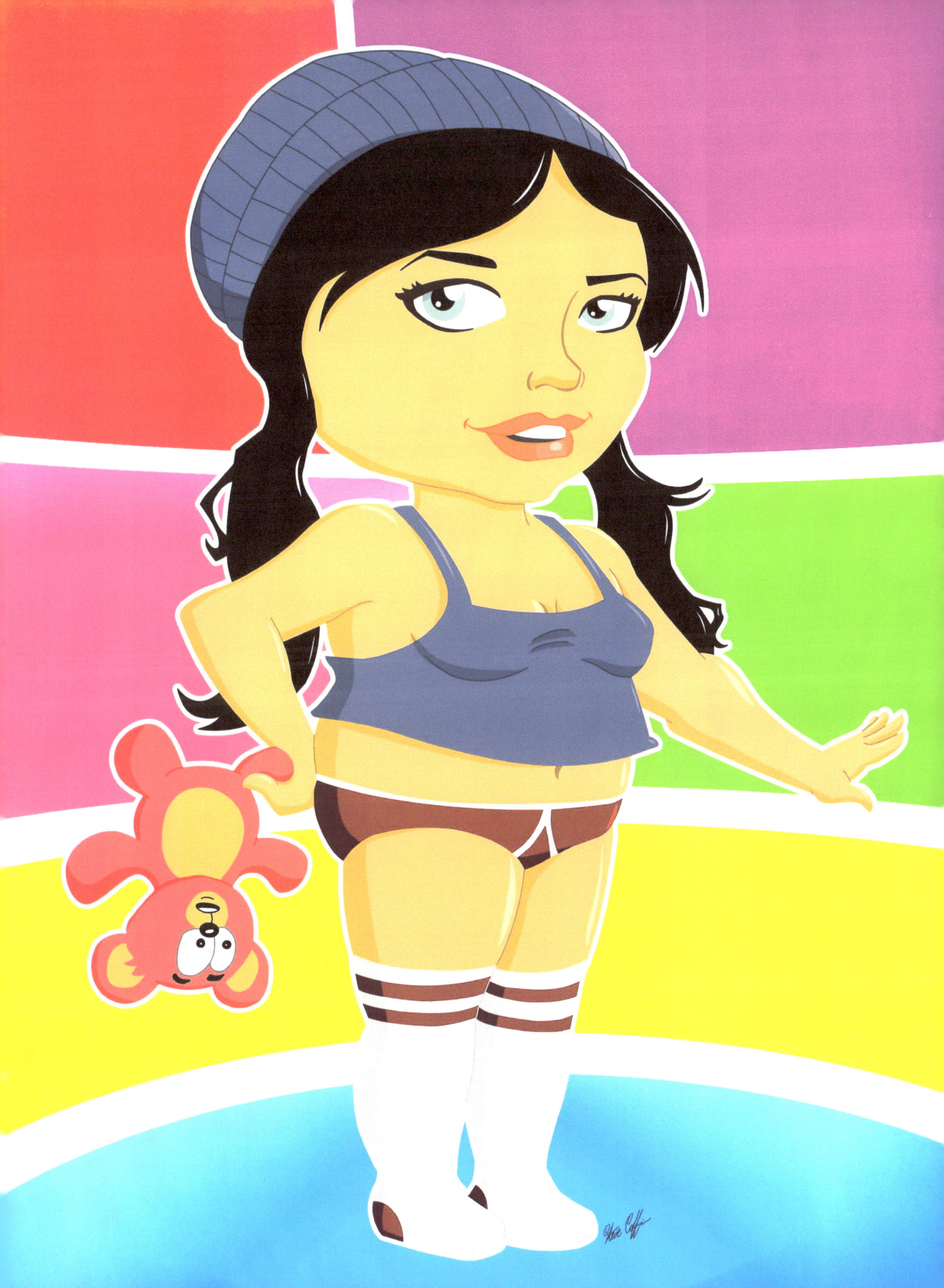

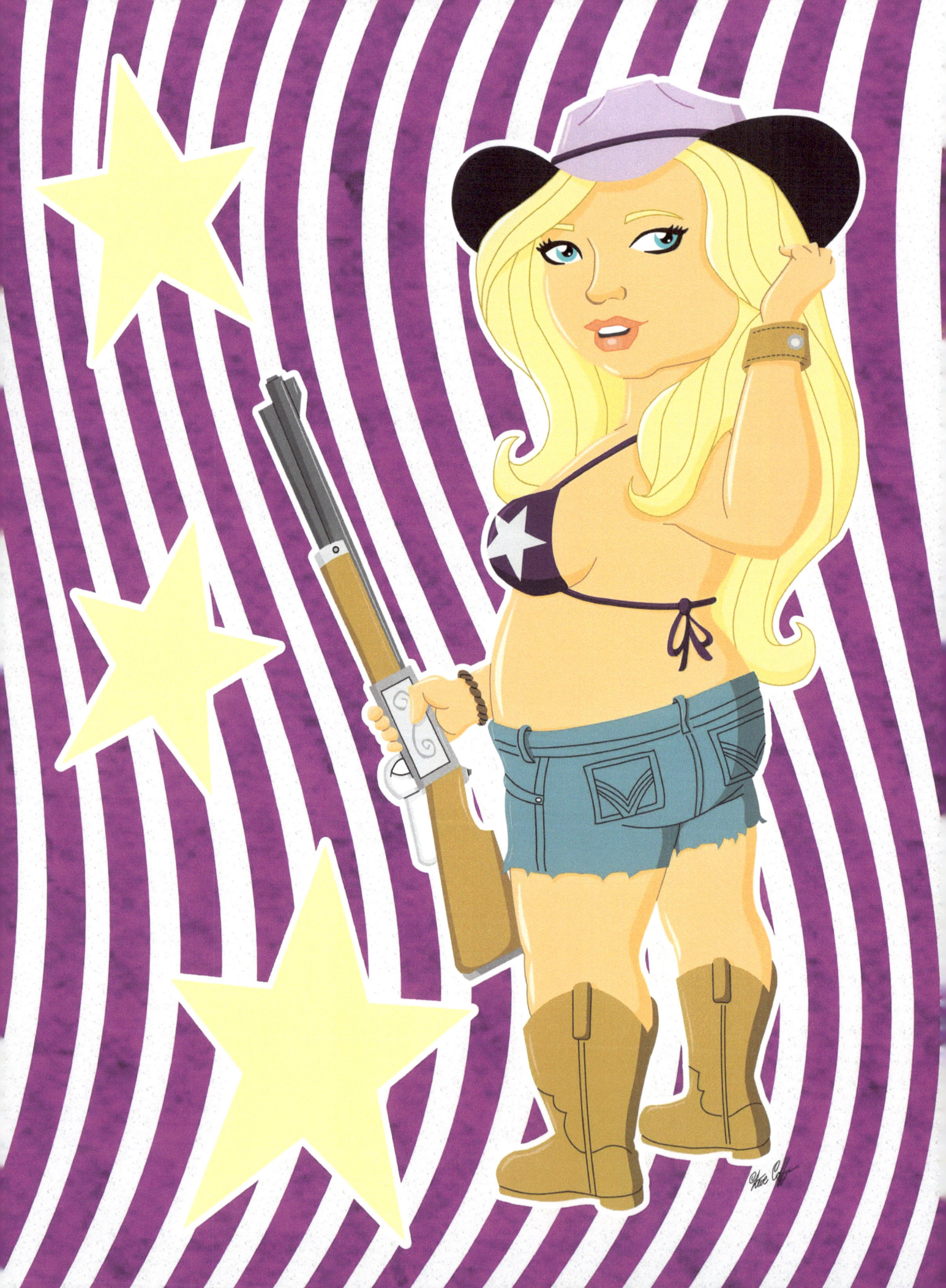

Let's Dance

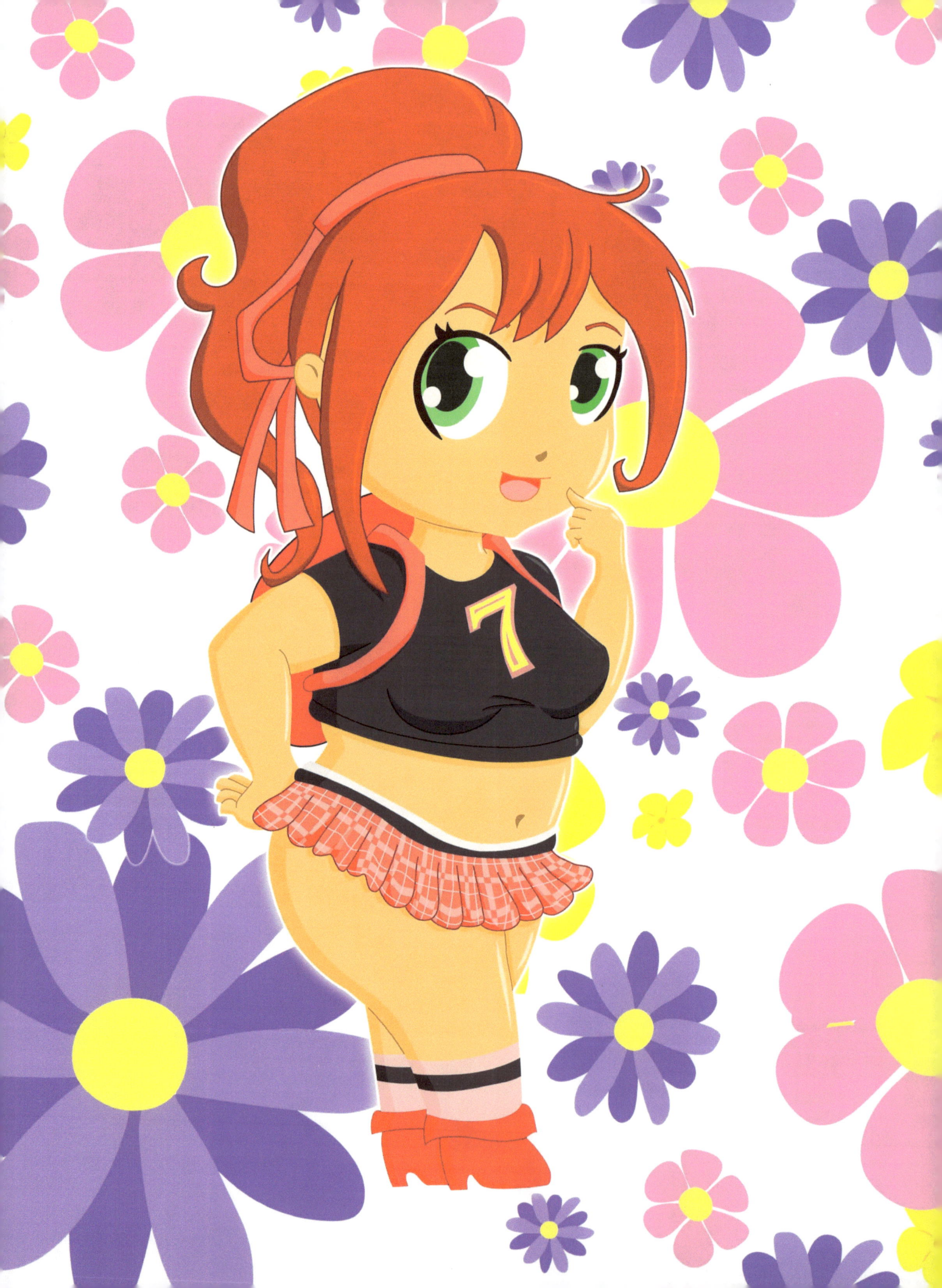

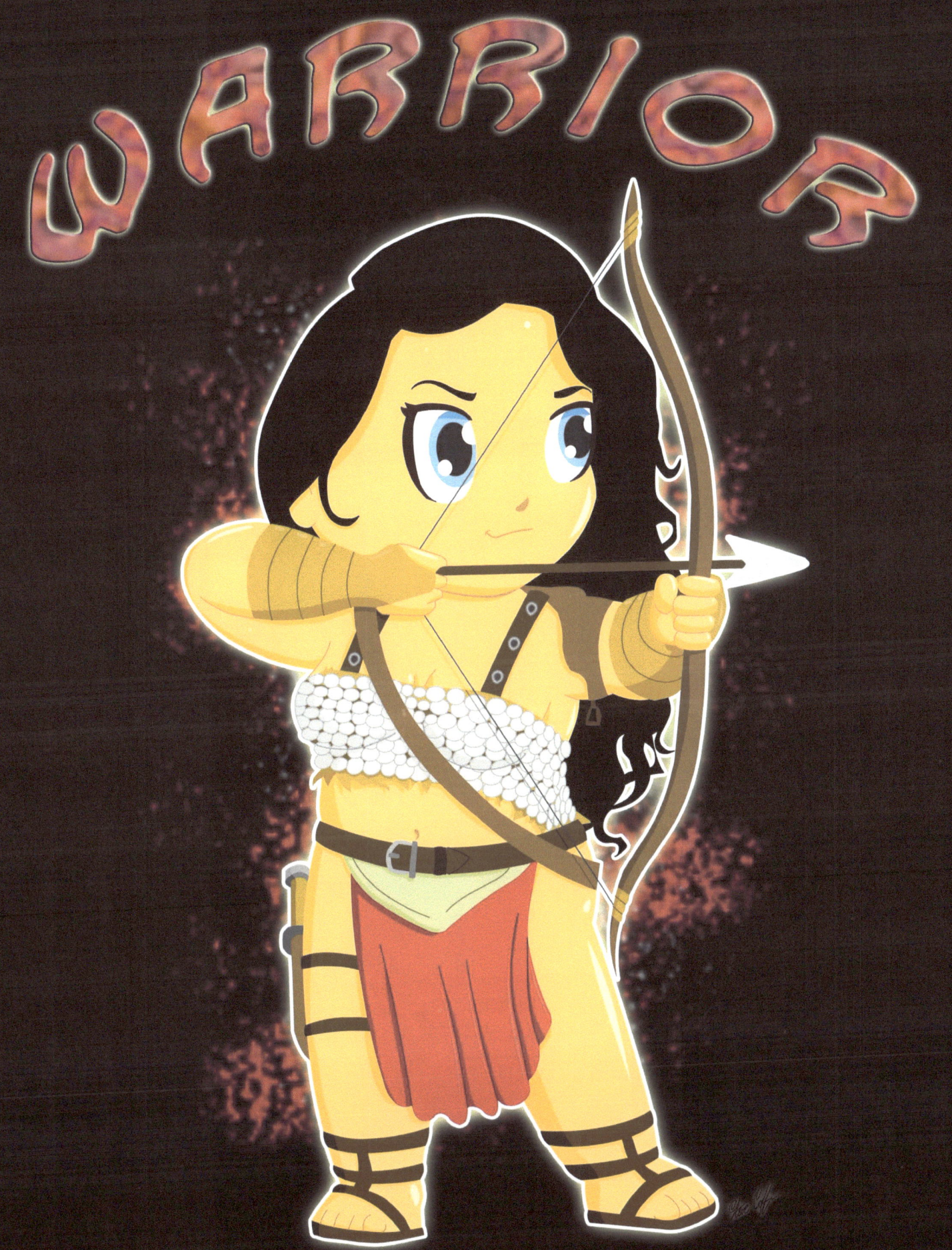

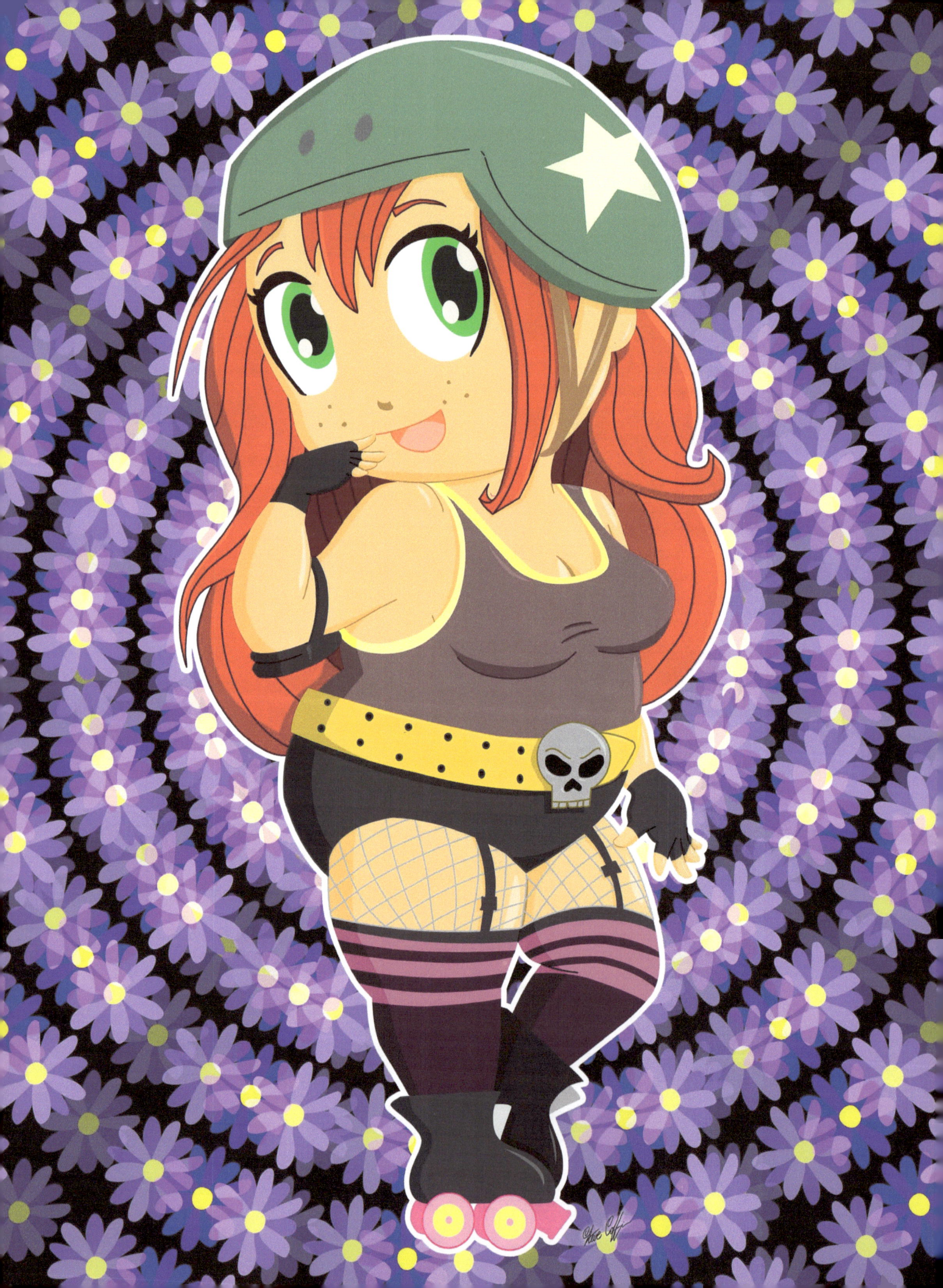

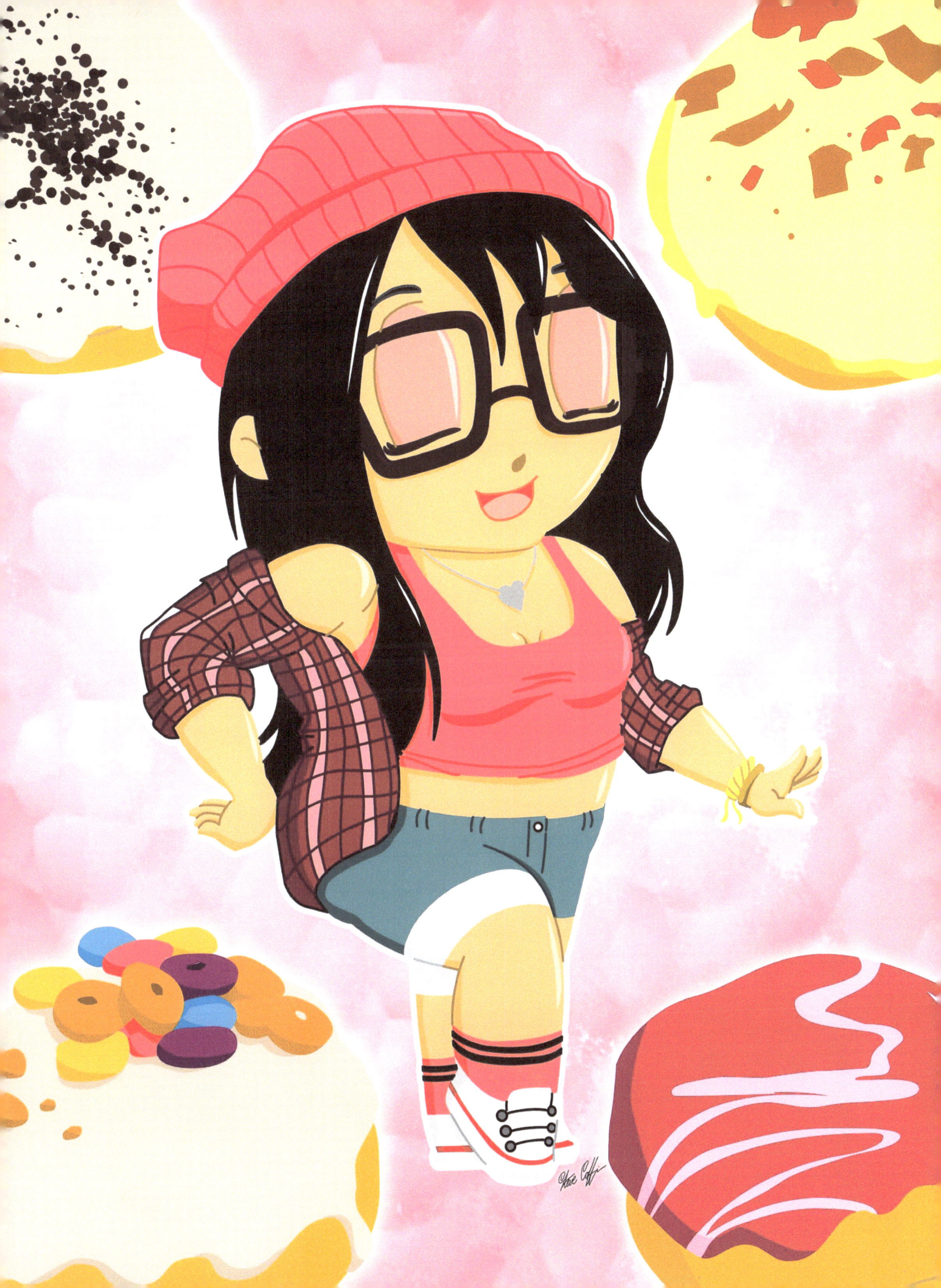

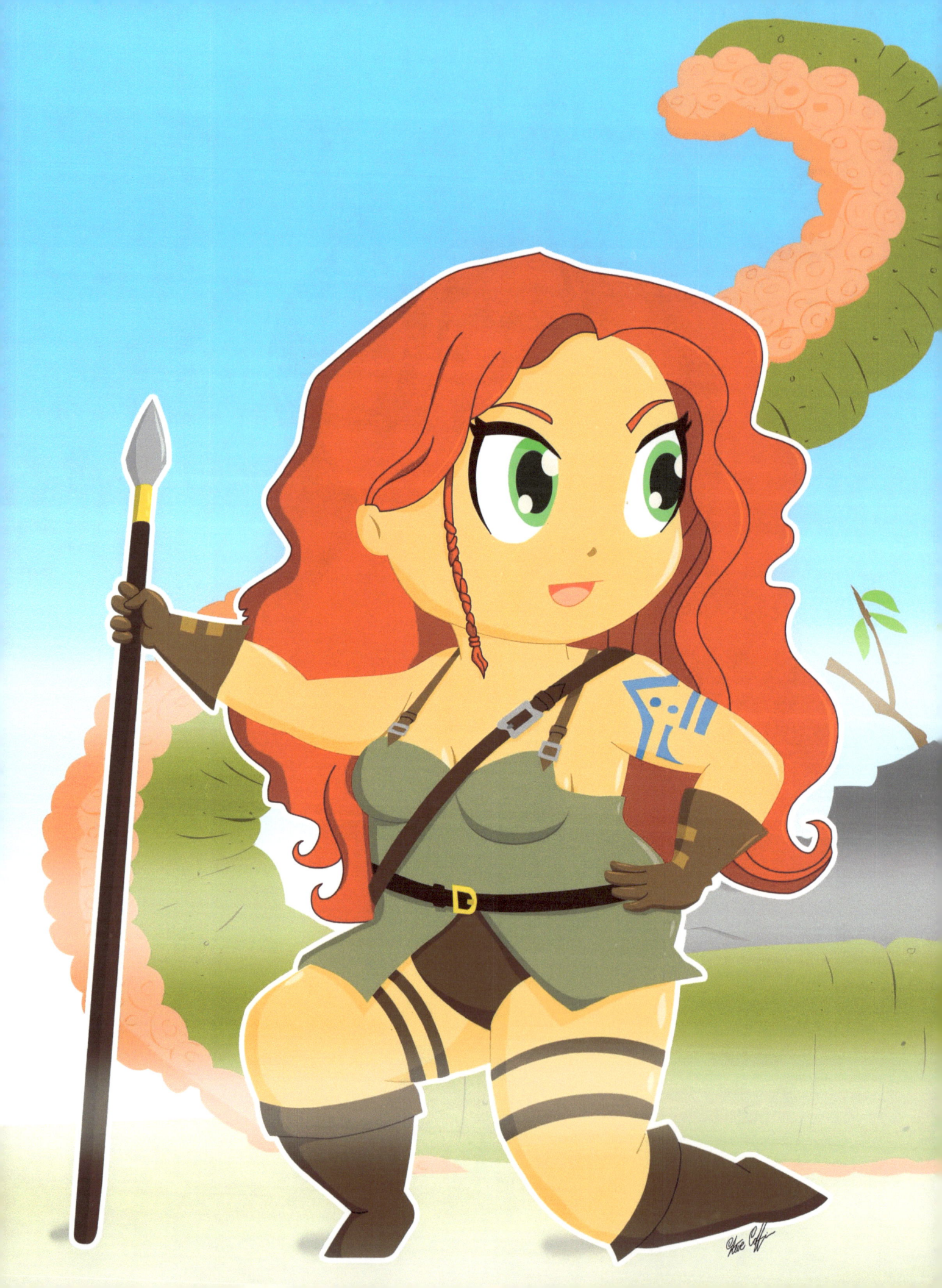

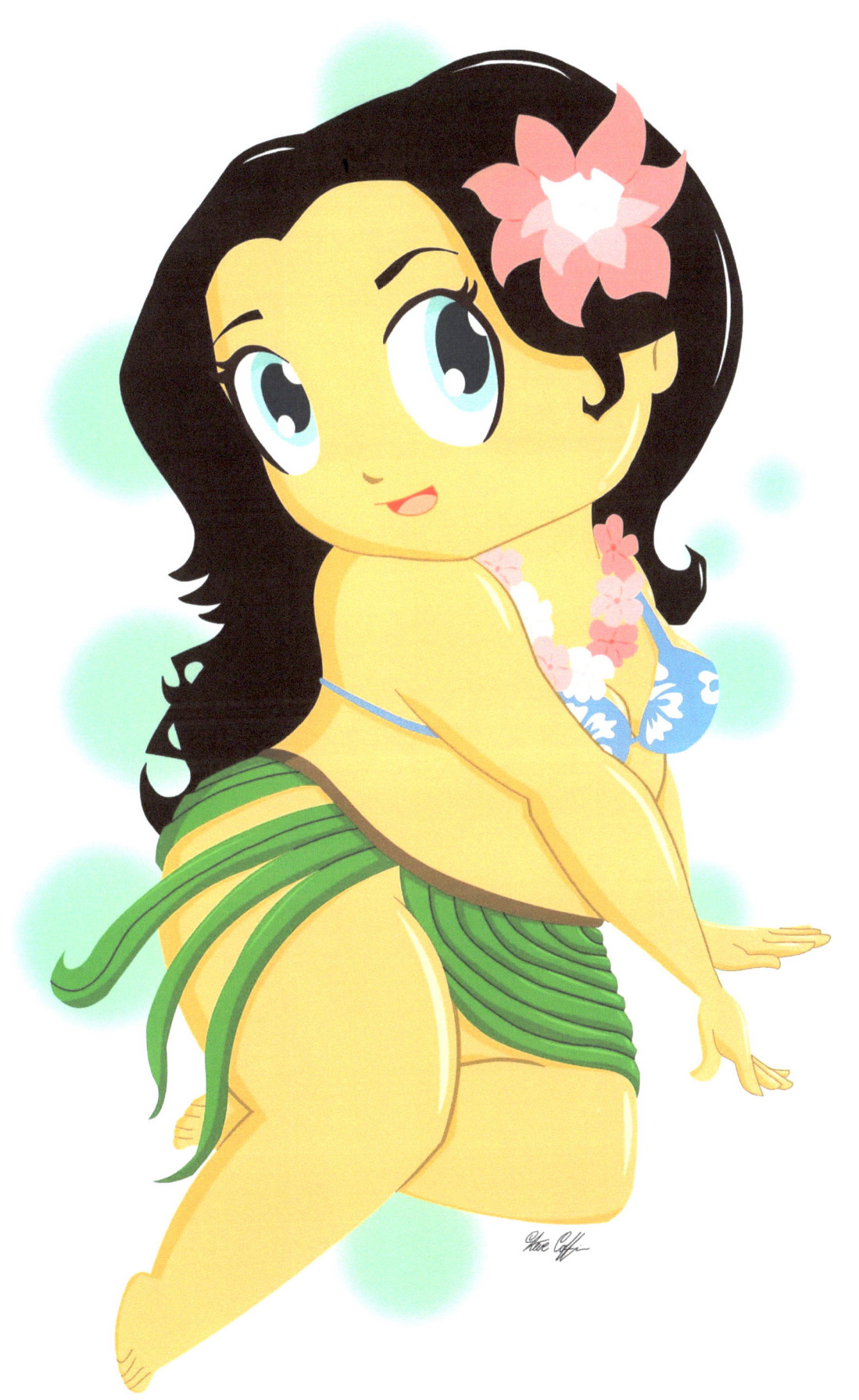

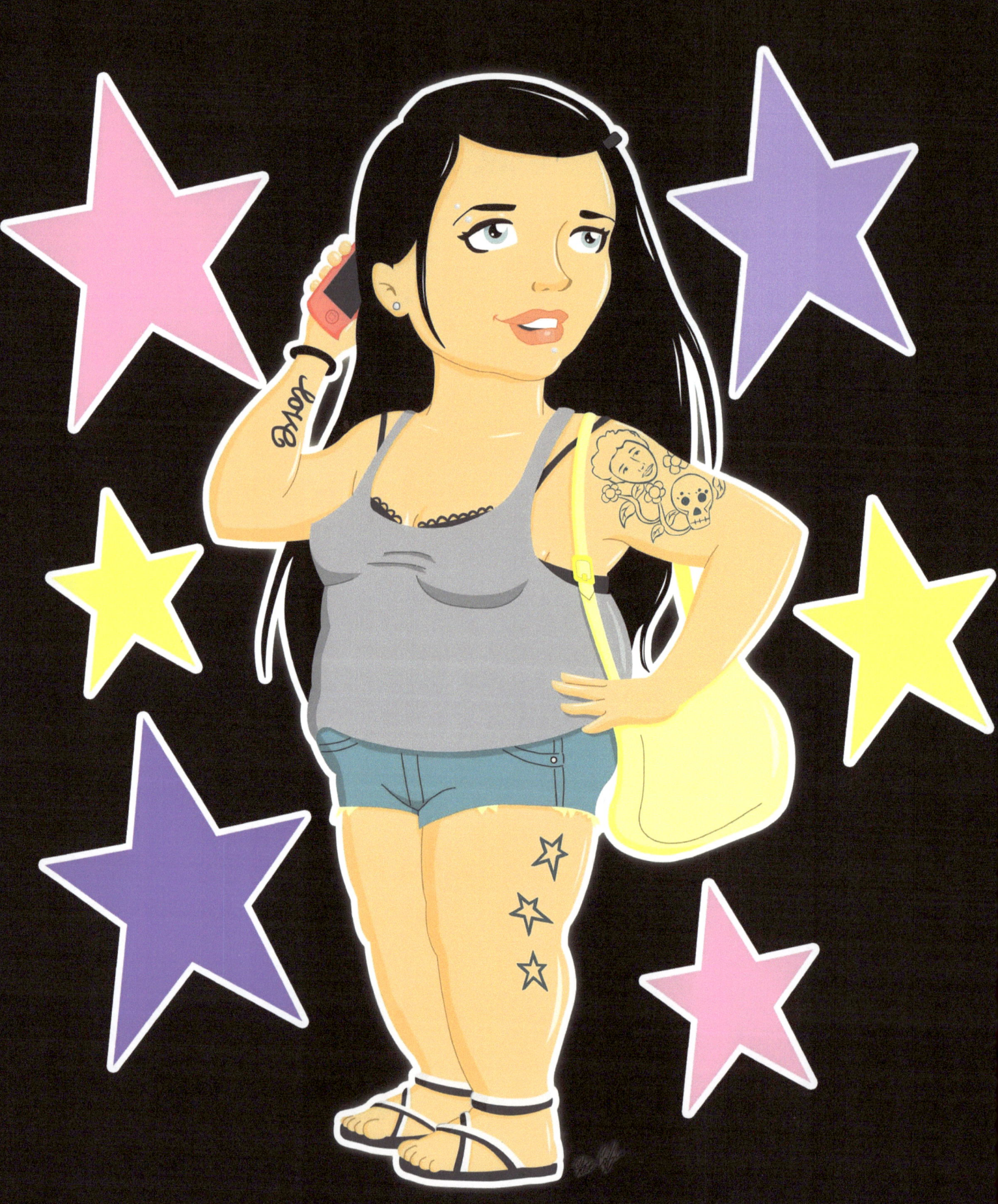

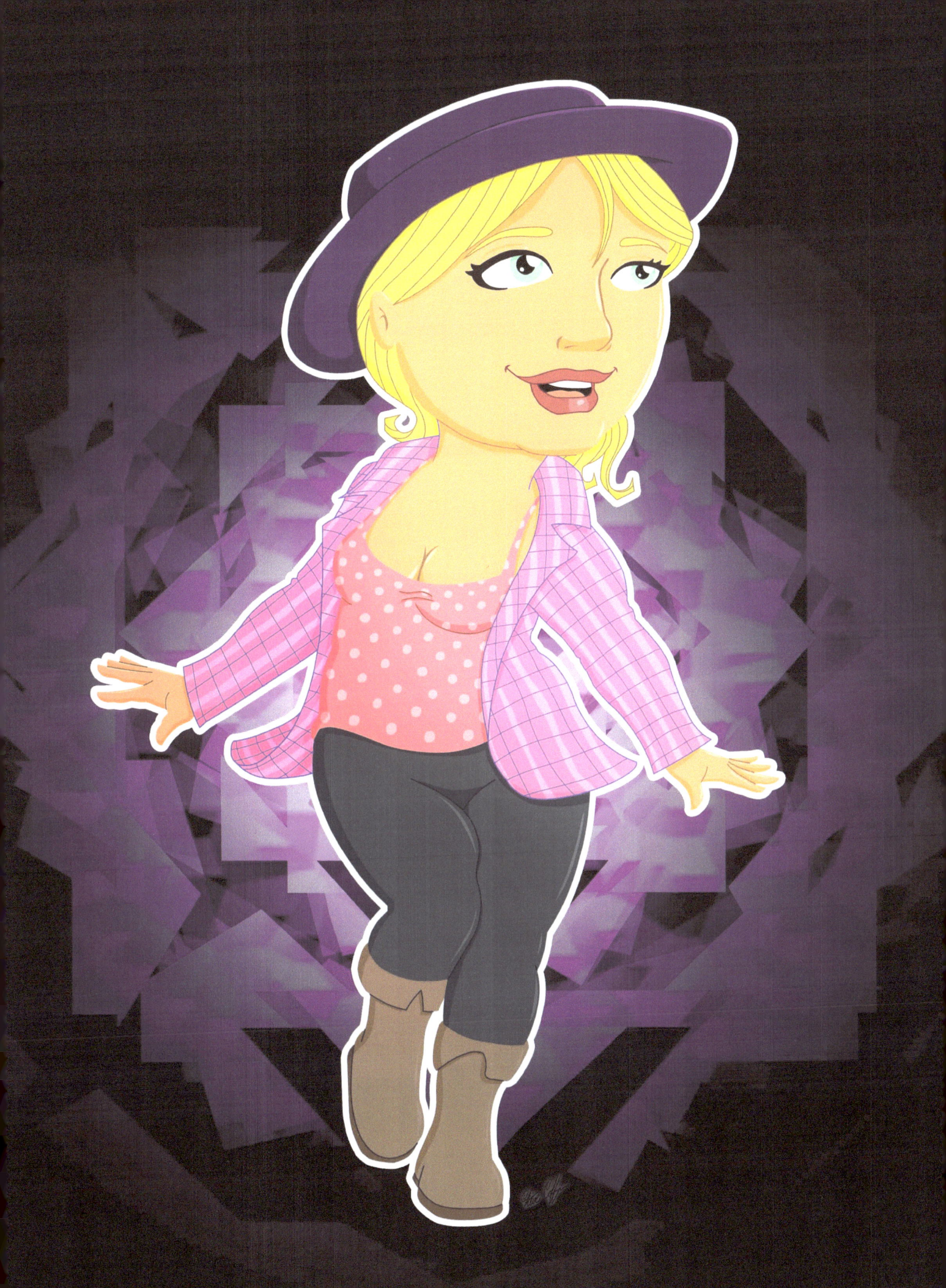

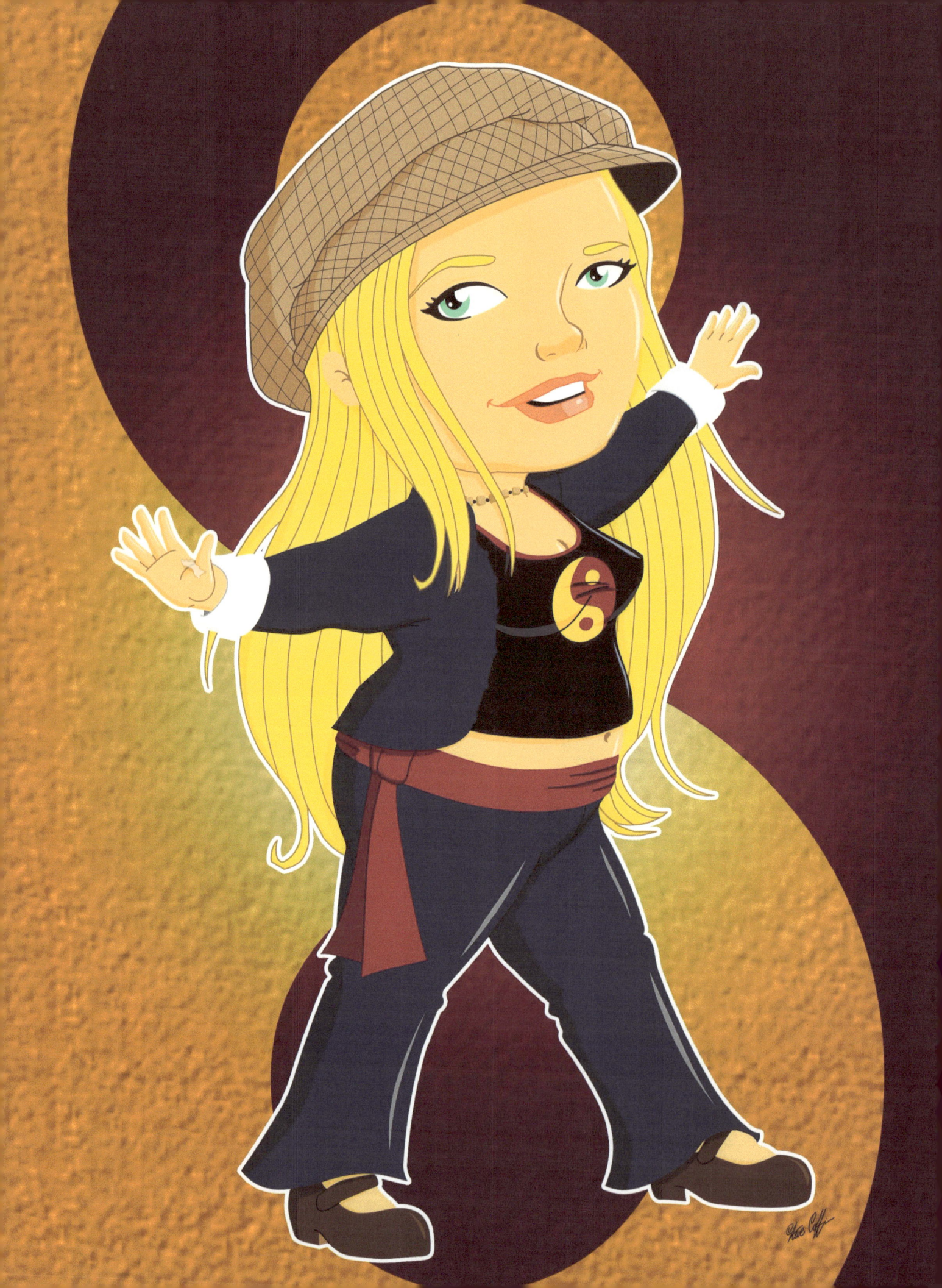

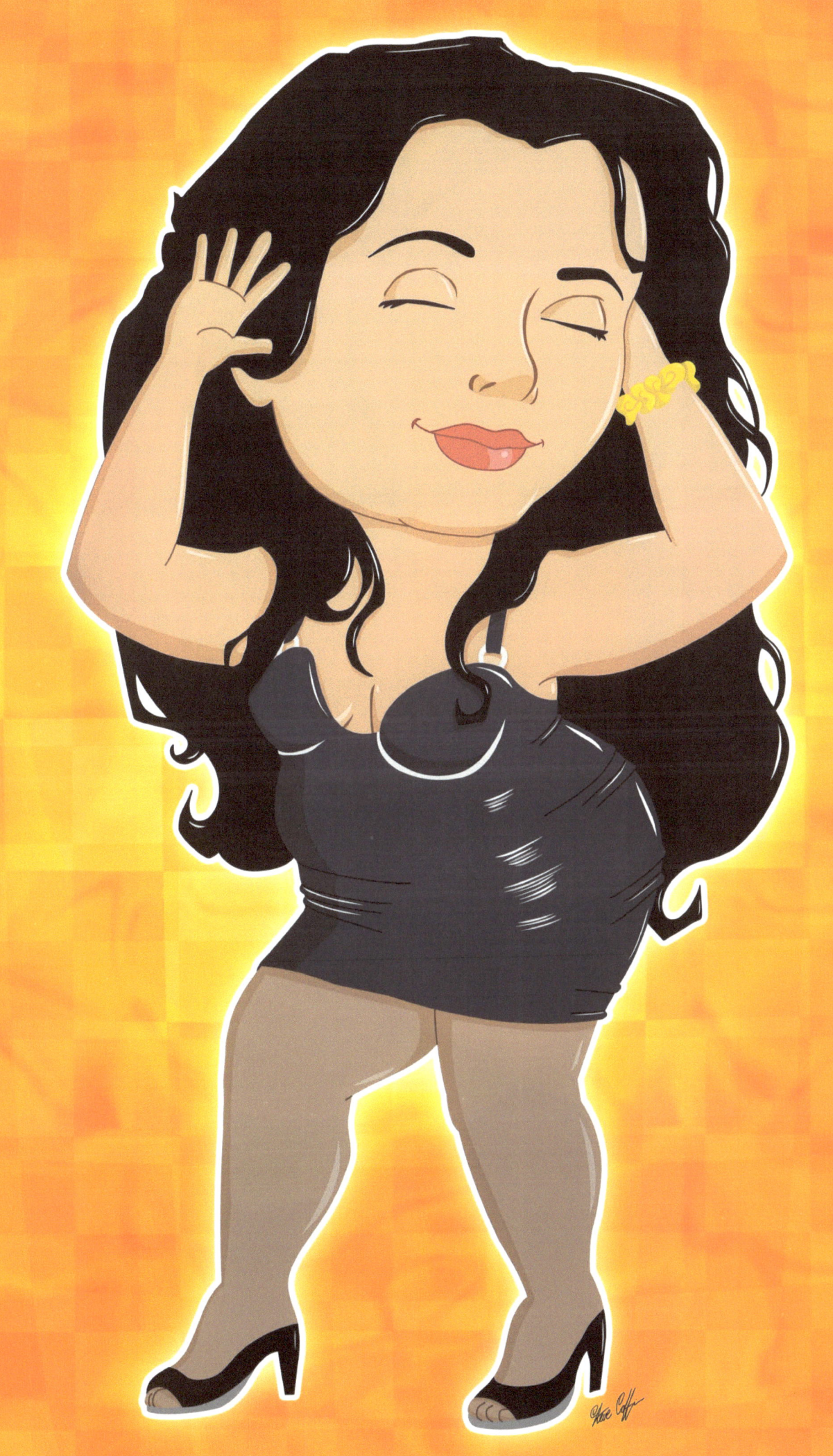

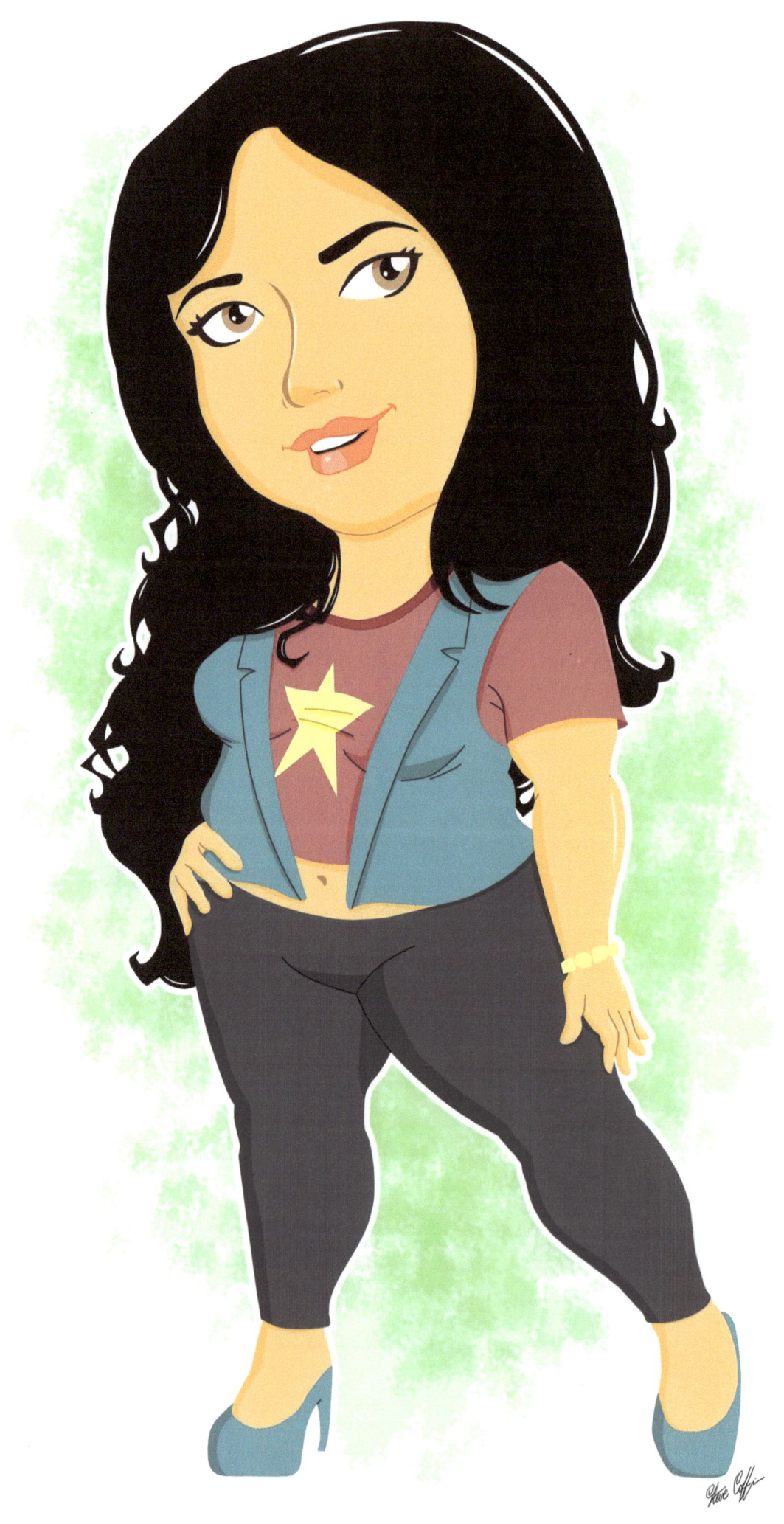

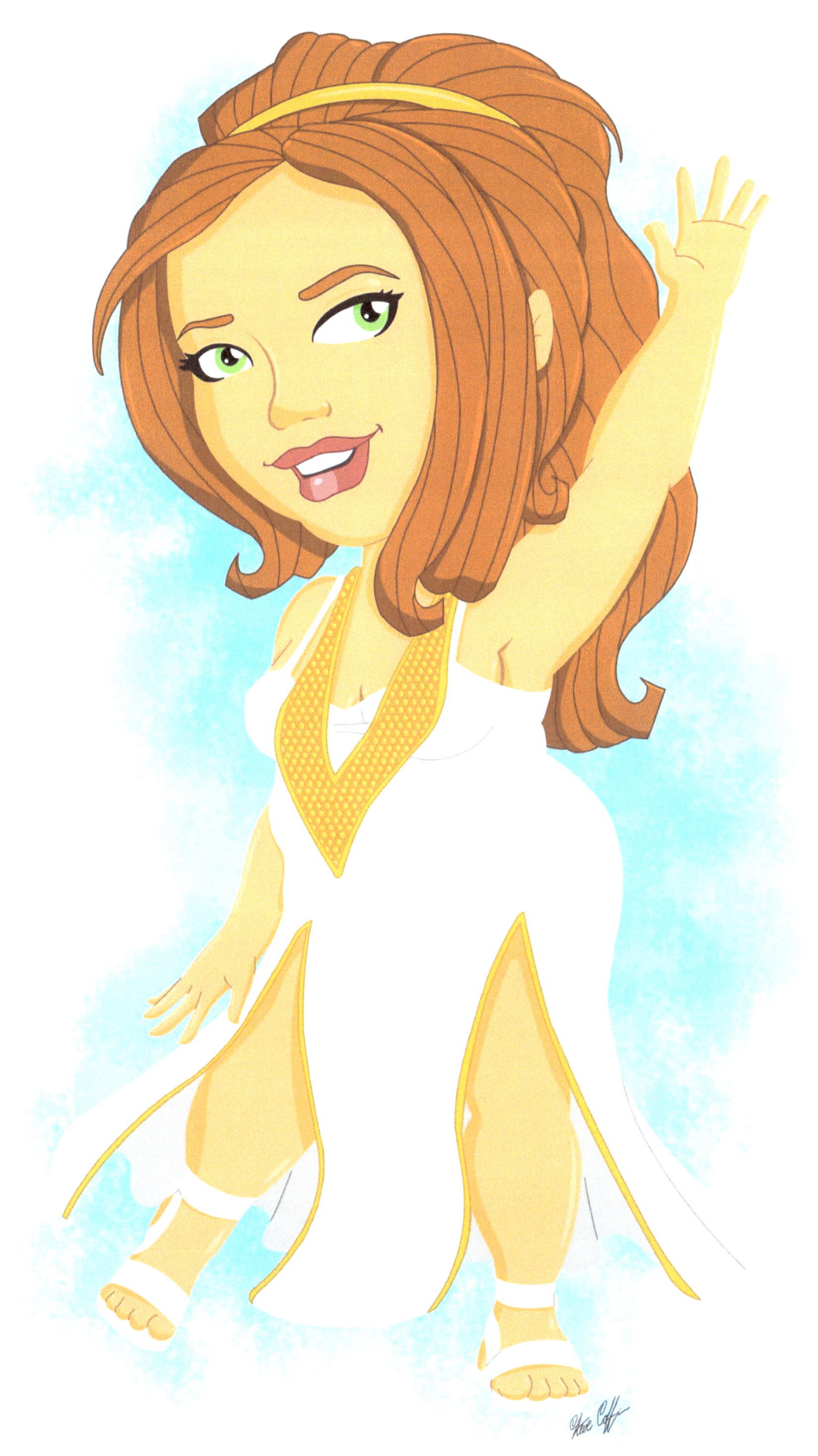

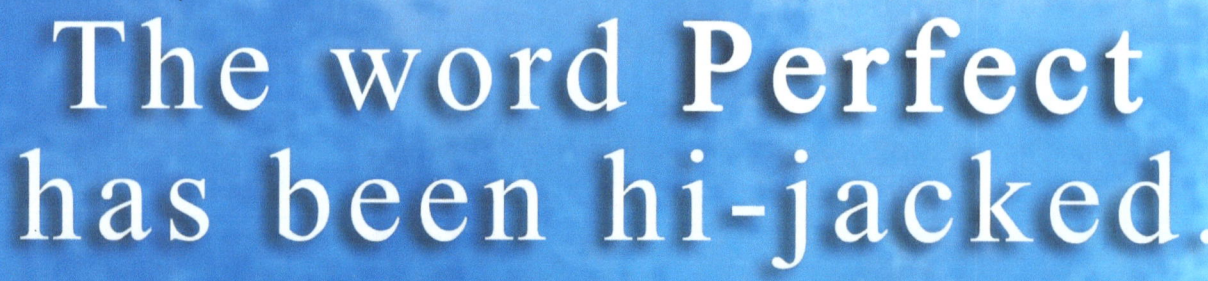

The word **Perfect** has been hi-jacked.
YOU ARE Perfect to start with..
You are the only example of you that there will ever be, and that makes you **unique**, and that **is** what makes **you** Perfect...

Steve Coffin 2016

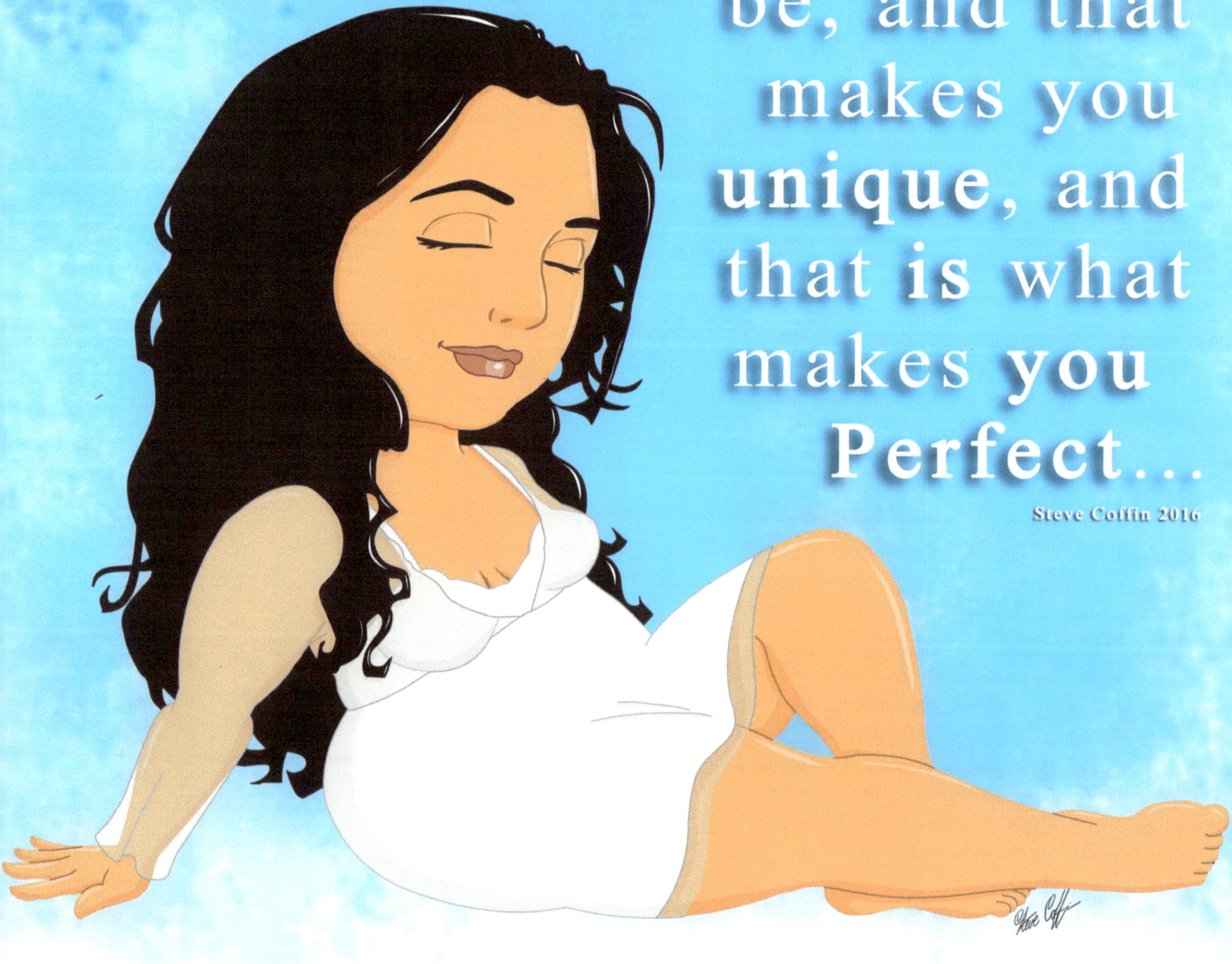

www.ingramcontent.com/pod-product-compliance
Lightning Source LLC
Chambersburg PA
CBHW050354180526
45159CB00005B/2014